ABINGDON PRESS   NEW YORK   NASHVILLE

EVERYTHING IS YOURS

G. Don Gilmore

EVERYTHING IS YOURS

EVERYTHING IS YOURS

Copyright © 1964 by Abingdon Press

Library of Congress Catalog Card Number: 64-16148

SET UP, PRINTED, AND BOUND BY
THE PARTHENON PRESS AT NASHVILLE,
TENNESSEE, UNITED STATES OF AMERICA

TO SUDY, LEIGH, DONNY

I have read in my children's eyes
truths that are hidden from the wise

Contents

Contents

1
Everything Is Yours

By so many roots as the marsh-grass sends in the sod
I will heartily lay me a-hold on the greatness of God.
—Sidney Lanier, "The Marshes of Glynn."

A critical situation had erupted in the newly founded church at Corinth. A petty quarrel had broken out that eventually succeeded in splitting the congregation into several factious groups. Each group organized itself around the name of a particular spiritual hero. "I belong to Paul . . . I belong to Cephas . . . I belong to Apollos." So divisive were these conflicting loyalties that common membership in the Church of Jesus Christ had nearly lost its significance.

The response of the apostle Paul to the Corinthian church's preoccupation with trivial disputes over irrelevent matters is a masterpiece in spiritual surgery. He lays bare the wound in his first letter to the Corinthians.

For while there is jealousy and strife among you, are you not of the flesh, and behaving like ordinary men? For when one says, "I belong to Paul," and another, "I belong to Apollos," are you not merely men? (I Cor. 3:3-4.)

Do you not know that you are God's temple and that God's Spirit dwells in you? If any one destroys God's temple, God

9

will destroy him. For God's temple is holy, and that temple you are. Let no one deceive himself. If any one among you thinks that he is wise in this age, let him become a fool that he may become wise. For the wisdom of this world is folly with God. For it is written, "He catches the wise in their craftiness," and again, "The Lord knows that the thoughts of the wise are futile." So let no one boast of men. For all things are yours, whether Paul or Apollos or Cephas or the world or life or death or the present or the future, all are yours; and you are Christ's; and Christ is God's. (I Cor. 3:16-23.)

"All things are yours," said Paul, with one qualifying consideration that gives meaning to the tremendous revelation that "you are Christ's." In other words everything is yours when you are in Christ.

This book is designed to probe the meaning of Paul's expansive statement, by describing how all things can be ours through the power of the Holy Spirit. In each chapter I shall attempt to magnify a facet of Paul's declaration, showing how "everything is yours" in terms of the "ministries of the churches," "the world," "life and death," and "the present and the future."

The mission of the Holy Spirit has always been to convict us of our sin, show us Christ, guide us into all truth, and clothe us with power. However, an enervating spiritual disease has sorely afflicted the Body of Christ in our day. Across the life of the Christian church it has become obvious that there is widespread pious mediocrity, growing spiritual dereliction, and an increasing lack of personal experience in Christ.

In the waking dilemma, large numbers of Christians

have become so preoccupied with pessimism for "the mess we're in" they have forgotten that man can be transformed by the work of the Holy Spirit. Equally tragic has been the downgrading of the supernatural power of God to the extent that many Christians really believe that the age of miracles, signs, and wonders must be limited to the biblical or apostolic era. In the following record I shall bear witness to the work of the Holy Spirit and to the fact that there can be such a thing as a contemporary book of Acts. Let us rediscover what belongs to us as we behold the gifts that are ours through the ministry of our risen Lord.

Immediately following his resurrection, Jesus told his followers not to depart from Jerusalem, but to wait for the promise of the Father, which, he said, "You heard from me" (Acts 1:4). He had promised, "I will pray the Father, and he will give you another Counselor, to be with you for ever" (John 14:16). "The Counselor, the Holy Spirit, whom the Father will send in my name, he will teach you all things" (John 14:26); "you shall receive power when the Holy Spirit has come upon you; and you shall be my witnesses in Jerusalem and in Judea and Samaria and to the end of the earth" (John 1:8).

So the entire Christian church gathered in an upper chamber in Jerusalem and waited. On the tenth day the course of human history was altered as God intervened in the affairs of men by baptizing 120 persons in his Holy Spirit. From the rush of a mighty wind new life filled them; tongues of fire rested above their heads reflecting the divine fire within; and, when they were filled to over-

11

flowing, their tongues were employed and the Holy Spirit began to speak through them in languages that were not their native tongues.

Before Pentecost those 120 Christians were trying with all their human resources to be the sort of persons Christ had wanted them to be, but they had discovered that by themselves it was absolutely impossible. After Pentecost they didn't need to try harder to be Christians; Christ through the Holy Spirit was living in them, prophesying through them, praising God through them, and bringing to their memory the remembrance of his teachings which at first they had not understood. God in the Holy Spirit literally changed the direction of human history.

Certain conditions remained unchanged, for the followers of Christ were still without wealth, influence, social position, prestige, government aid, and institutional backing. They were still uneducated folk without Bibles, Christian literature, or even a church. They continued to be despised, rejected, persecuted, and subjected to forced labor and death. Everything appeared to be against them except for one thing—they had been baptized in the Holy Spirit, and the presence of God was dwelling in them. Within seventy years, according to the most conservative estimate, there were half a million followers of Christ in the world.

Sane people today are worried about the condition of world affairs. You do not need to be a reader of contemporary fiction, a theologian, philosopher, crime expert, sociologist, or psychologist to realize the world is rapidly slipping back into the sort of condition that prevailed when Christ came in the flesh. Someone has called this "an age of universal corruption."

There is only one power that can change this world, and it is the power of God working through the Holy Spirit, baptizing churches into a deep, profound experience of God. It is sad that so few people are aware of his presence and, more important, his power.

Think of it! If all the resources available to the modern Christian church—such as government approval, public sentiment, unbelievable wealth, established institutions and organizations, the Scriptures and Christian literature printed in every language and dialect—were consecrated to the guidance and direction of the Holy Spirit, the whole world would belong to Christ within a decade. I do not consider the preceding statement an exaggeration and shall stand on it.

The average church member is scarcely aware of what the Holy Spirit is, let alone what he can do; therefore he naturally turns to agencies, programs, culture, oratory, and church machinery to overcome his spiritual barrenness. Many church members are like those disciples in Ephesus. Paul said to them, "Did you receive the Holy Spirit when you believed?" And they said, "No, we have never even heard that there is a Holy Spirit" (Acts 19:2).

Perhaps a little background information at this point might prove helpful. The Bible is filled with allusions to God's Spirit. As Randolph S. Foster used to say: "It breathes in the prophecy, thunders in the law, murmurs in the narratives, whispers in the promises, supplicates in the prayers, sparkles in the poetry, resounds in the songs, speaks in the types, glows in the imagery, voices in the language, and burns in the spirit of the whole scheme, from the alpha to the omega, from its beginning to its end." [1]

The Holy Spirit is a distinctively New Testament expression. In the Old Testament we find allusions to "the Spirit of God," and "the Spirit of the Lord," but the Holy Spirit as such is not mentioned and for a very good reason. There could never be a Holy Spirit until men would see the holy quality of a life filled with God's Spirit. In Jesus Christ the Spirit of God becomes flesh, and from that time on we can define the nature of God's Holy Spirit. In the Old Testament, God's Spirit was synonymous with the spirit of war and vengeance. In the New Testament, God's son revealed that the spirit of God is transforming love, creative power, and dynamic holiness. Therefore, our concept of holiness in Holy Spirit is shaped by, and consonant with, what we know of Jesus Christ.

The Holy Spirit is a person, not a vague spirit but a spiritual person. People are often confused by the trinitarian idea of God as Father, Son, and Holy Spirit, three in one, and much time has been spent trying to fathom this formula. Our real problem is that we have an inadequate supply of words available for the purpose of giving symbolic meaning to spiritual reality. We seek to identify God as Creator, so we borrow a descriptive name, the name Jesus gave him, and call him "Father." We seek to identify God as he revealed himself in the

[1] A. M. Hills, *Holiness and Power* (Cincinnati: Revivalist Press 1897), p. 293.

14

flesh, so again we borrow the word of Jesus and we call him the "Son." We seek to identify God as he lives and moves and has his being in our lives, and again borrowing from Jesus Christ we speak of God as the "Holy Spirit."

Therefore all the knowledge we have of God, the Holy Spirit, the Trinity, and truth itself is to be found first of all in our knowledge of Jesus Christ. And Jesus Christ is who he is because, as he said: "The Spirit of the Lord is upon me, because he has anointed me" (Luke 4:18). God, through his Spirit, anointed Jesus to be the Christ, meaning "anointed one.") "Let all the house of Israel therefore know assuredly that God has made him both Lord and Christ, this Jesus whom you crucified." (Acts 2:36.) And the Spirit of God, now through Jesus Christ, the Holy Spirit, will not call attention to himself but will speak only of Jesus Christ. Jesus said, "When the Spirit of truth comes, he will guide you into all the truth; for he will not speak on his own authority. . . . He will glorify me" (John 16:13, 14). Jesus Christ remains the key to our knowledge of God, the Holy Spirit, the Trinity, and truth itself.

I am not a member of a Pentecostal or Holiness church, but I am convinced that their emphasis on the baptism of the Holy Spirit is the most important Christian teaching on the face of the earth today. Henry P. Van Dusen has said, "The Holy Spirit has always been troublesome to church officialdom because he does seem to be unruly, unpredictable and radical." Dr. Van Dusen has termed the work of the Holy Spirit as "his sovereign unpredictability." Karl Barth has said, "A presupposed spirit is certainly not the Holy Spirit, and a theology that presumes to have it under control can only be unspiritual theology." Carl Henry, of *Christianity Today,* has aptly called the Holy Spirit in the twentieth century "a displaced person."

The contemporary spirit of pessimism and hopelessness has more deeply penetrated the heart of the church than any of us realize, and with profoundly disturbing consequences. The church has grown accustomed to wearing the spiritless gray flannel clothing of the society in which it resides. Slowly but surely the church has become institutionalized, self-perpetuating, self-worshiping, afraid to violate institutional proprieties and world values. Sooner or later it will come to the point of no return where, even if it so desired, it could not escape the responsibilities of marriage to the secular standards it has adopted. When the Holy Spirit is dismissed as a fairy tale; when the Bible loses its authority as the Word of God; when sin loses its sting in the Christian's conscience; when goodness becomes a compensating adjective, and moral and spiritual laws become a set of aesthetic rules for nice manners, then the church has lost the saving power of her Lord. No wonder the church is lapsing into a theological doctrine of man's depravity and God's transcendance, never the twain to meet, as though this is the answer to the dilemma.

But Paul, full of the Holy Spirit, cried out in his day, and the sound of that voice must be heard in ours: "All things are yours . . . and you are Christ's; and Christ is God's." Jesus said, "I will pray the Father, and he will give you another Counselor [the Holy Spirit], to be with you for ever, even the Spirit of truth, whom the world cannot receive, because it neither sees him nor knows him; you know him, for he dwells with you, and will be in you" (John 14:16-17).

The unspoken question before the church today is whether or not we are treating the Holy Spirit as the person of God. There seems to be a general hesitancy among many church people to believe that God, through the Holy Spirit, can accomplish the mighty works in our day that are recorded in the New Testament.

I do not want to convey the impression that church people today do not have faith in God—they do. But they do not have the power of God which can come only through the Holy Spirit—that "displaced person" of the church. Powerless church members, when attempting to witness for Christ without personal experience of him, will quote dozens of secondhand authorities, but their hearers will remain unmoved and unhelped. Powerless church members, after running out of worthwhile projects to sustain their religious enthusiasm, inevitably decide that the only thing left to do is construct a new sanctuary or build a church-school plant.

Powerless churches have embarked on programs of culturizing the congregation—art shows, musical reviews, dramatic presentations—in order to regain their lost vitality; but this is not what they really need, and after the sound and fury is past they are just as empty as before.

Three fourths of our churches today are simply dried-up religious societies, functioning for no higher purpose than the promotion of religious satisfaction among the members and those few who once a week happen to drop by to see what's going on. It is not good, bad, or indif-

17

ferent programs and organizational activity that will meet the needs of these people. Only the church filled with the Holy Spirit is sufficient. Only God can raise up the dead bones of the modern-day church.

One evening I went with a friend to visit a man who is not a member of our church. The nonmember's wife, who had promoted the visit, met us at the door and explained that her husband was hiding in the basement. He had no desire to talk to us about the church, church membership, doctrine, beliefs, etc. I tried to explain to the man's wife that we had not come to discuss any of these things. She simply shrugged her shoulders and pointed toward the basement. With that we made our way through the kitchen to the basement door and marched down the steps. We found our man perched on a table in the gathering darkness of his sanctuary, now violated by strangers. For a solid hour we told him what Christ is doing in our lives, and gave him personal testimony concerning the works of the Holy Spirit. Never once did we mention church membership, denominational public relations, or hard doctrine. Taken by surprise, he listened in rapt attention and even volunteered a few comments of his own. I am sure he never expected to be involved in a discussion on Christ and the Holy Spirit. At the close of our time together he followed us up the basement stairs. This is what people are hungry for, the witness of God's Holy Spirit in action and to know that it is available to each one of us.

Hunger for the Holy Spirit persists in the lives of Christians, but most of them are not aware of why they feel hungry. Turning in every direction to explain their leanness, they say, "We are reading the best books, studying the Bible, praying, going to church, but something is missing."

In 1956 David DuPlessis addressed a group of American ecumenical leaders. After he had given his talk, one man approached the great spiritual leader and said: "Please tell us the difference between you and us. We quote the same scriptures as you do, and yet when you say those words they sound different. We say the same things that you do, but there seems to be a deeper implication in what you say. You have said nothing with which we differ and yet there seems to be a distinct difference somewhere." DuPlessis replied, "Gentlemen, comparisons are odious and I do not wish to injure anyone's feelings or hurt your pride. But the truth as I see it is this; you have the truth on ice and I have it on fire. My friends, if you will take the great truths of the gospel out of your theological deep freezers and get them on fire with the Holy Spirit, your church will yet turn the world upside down. The church does not need better theologians but rather men full of faith and the Holy Spirit."

The unmistakable need of the church today is for the individual Christian to halt in his tracks, develop his spiritual receptivity in prayer, and receive the Holy Spirit. We must first enter a place where we will not be disturbed in our quest. Through disciplined use of the Bible, hymnal, and other devotional materials we kindle the responsiveness of our being. Then we speak to God, praying that his Holy Spirit will enter us and manifest himself through us. We should not petition for a specific gift such as tongues, healing, prophecy, preaching, teaching, apostleship, or interpretation of tongues; rather we should seek the Giver of all the gifts, and the Holy Spirit will bless us with the appropriate gift with which to praise God.

The Holy Spirit may begin to speak through you as it happened to a discouraged Frank Laubach on the island of Mindanao in the Philippines when he had failed in his missionary work with the fierce Moros Indians. He cried out to God, "Why did you send me to this terrible place among these thieving, murdering, hateful people?" He received his answer one night while praying on Signal Hill. Dr. Laubach tells it this way:

One night as I was praying my lips began to talk to me and they said to me, "Frank, they don't love you because you don't love them. You look down on them with your white man's sense of superiority. You think because you are educated as a Christian and a white man that you are better than they are and they can read you like a book. If you would only love them as I love them they'd love you back." [2]

That was the night that changed Frank Laubach's life.

Who knows what the Holy Spirit may move you to do. He is always unpredictable. You may speak in another language, or be able to speak for the Holy Spirit in your own language. You may receive the gift of healing, of prophecy, or one of the other gifts, but in every case the gift is given to glorify God.

It is a shame that many Christians have been trained to draw a line through most of the spiritual gifts because

[2] From a tape recording made by Frank Laubach, at Groesbeck Methodist Church, Cincinnati, Ohio, May 21, 1962.

they do not fit their theological notions. But how can we dismiss with such cavalier disdain that which is repeated over and over again in the New Testament? For instance, can we find justifiable grounds for accusing Paul of lunacy because he often mentioned the gift of tongues? And if we do so, are we not begging the logical inference that two thirds of the New Testament was written by a man who (1) didn't know what he was talking about; (2) didn't know what he said; or (3) didn't mean what he said?

While I cannot judge the spiritual response of others, I still am repelled by the wild emotionalism associated with receiving the gift of the Holy Spirit. To me the gifts of the Spirit are given for the direct edification of the church, and more particularly for private devotions, and are not to be displayed like merchandise in the public marketplace. However, we are not to judge the Holy Spirit by the way some people respond to him. In the case of tongue speaking, Paul admonishes that we are not to put on a show for others. He writes, "For one who speaks in a tongue speaks not to men but to God" (I Cor. 14:2). "All things should be done decently and in order." (I Cor. 14:40.)

Long under the cloud of intellectual suspicion, the gift of tongues has only recently become an acceptable subject for polite conversation among church people. The following statement appeared in *The Living Church,* an independent Episcopal weekly:

Speaking in tongues is no longer a phenomenon of some odd sect across the street. It is in our midst and it is being

21

practiced by clergy and laity who have stature and good reputations in the church. Its widespread introduction would jar against our esthetic sense and some of our strongly entrenched preconceptions. But we know that we are members of a church that definitely needs jarring.

In 1960 the Commission on Faith and Order of the World Council of Churches drafted an amazing prayer guide under the title *Week of Prayer for Christian Unity*. The eighth-day devotional is as follows:

Eighth Day

And God has appointed in the church . . . speakers in tongues and interpreters.

Read Acts 2:4-11, and Genesis 40:5-8.
As you pray, think of the meaning of these verses as they apply to your own particular congregation, remembering the significance of the unusual and extraordinary in the Christian church as opposed to the normal and mediocre.
—of the witness which does not come only from the intellect and transcends the understanding of man
—of the need for interpretation and expression as well as for language that can be understood everywhere and by all
—of "speakers in tongues" who continually challenge and disturb the church which all too easily becomes complacent and self-satisfied and contented to remain as it is.
As you pray, remember that you are a member of the whole Body of Christ and reflect on the place within the Body of those individuals and groups which do not fit easily or comfortably into the present ecclesiastical and ecumenical patterns.

22

The glossolalia or speaking in tongues has long been recognized as the central manifestation of the Holy Spirit in the Pentecostal churches. In recent years this phenomenon has blossomed forth in the historic denominational churches as well.

Those who speak in tongues say that the gift of the Holy Spirit gives them a deeper communion with God as they praise him in a language that is not native to them. No egoism or rational prohibition can enter this praising of God because the conscious mind does not understand what is being said. This is truly a deep calling to the deep. Therefore, if someone who speaks in a tongue wishes to know what he is saying, then he needs to secure the services of an interpreter. Concerning the glossolalia in church Paul stated, "If the question of speaking with a tongue arises, confine the speaking to two or three at the most and have someone to interpret what is said" (I Cor. 14:27, Phillips).

Some of the languages that are said to be generally spoken are Greek, Hebrew, Italian, Aramaic, and Chinese dialect. In most instances the manifestation of speaking in tongues occurs when someone in deep communion with the Holy Spirit lays his hands on the head of the seeker of this gift. Suddenly the seeker has the ability to speak or sing in a language with which he has had no previous experience. "The tongue" in most cases is heard as a fluent, controlled combination of words and sounds.

Those who oppose this tongue-speaking movement say that whenever the glossolalia springs up it creates divisions, dissensions, fear and a general uneasy feeling. It

23

accomplishes nothing of any significance and generally works a disadvantage in the life of the local church.

A chief danger in this movement is the self-righteous, authoritative, "we have the only truth" attitude that can do great harm to the witness of the Spirit. Another pitfall might be that people will be seeking a gift instead of Jesus Christ, the giver of the gifts.

In his address before a diocesan convention on January 29, 1963, Francis Eric Bloy, Episcopal Bishop of Los Angeles, said:

I would give a particular word of caution to those among us who have received the gift of tongues. Be very wise and extremely careful how you exercise this gift. Be humble and charitable and not overzealous in your witnessing before others, as to the reality of your gift. Remember always, that one does not have to receive the gift of tongues to partake of salvation in Christ, or to witness faithfully and effectively to His truth.

There is a cheap form of emotional exhibitionism, that goes hand in hand with speaking in tongues, which is a menace to the life of the church. I have seen unbalanced people take this beautiful gift of the Spirit and employ it for the purpose of neurotic release before an unsuspecting congregation. What they are doing in the "name of the Lord" is in actuality a satanic device for scattering the flock of Christ. Churches that are truly filled with the Holy Spirit share glorious testimony to the harmony of a balanced experience in Christ.

John MacKay, past president of the Princeton Theological Seminary, has said, "One of our serious troubles of the church today is that it has become legitimate to be emotional in anything but religion. The need is for something that will summon one's whole enthusiasm. . . . The moment the church becomes completely programized, it becomes a monument to God's memory and not an instrument of his living power."

Dare we make the journey back to Pentecost? Here I am not speaking of any one denomination but all Christian people. John Wesley discovered this need. He had studied and reasoned his way through the Christian faith, but he still hungered with a divine discontent. Later he wrote, "My brother Charles and I reading the Bible, saw we could not be saved without holiness." Still later he saw that this holiness comes by faith, and that men are justified before they are sanctified; but still holiness was his object, inward and outward holiness. God then thrust them out to raise up a holy people. The holiness that Wesley spoke of is the transforming power received in the baptism of the Holy Spirit.

However, he warned others that those who seek after this sort of holiness will be sneered at, criticized, and "hooted at like mad dogs."

The early Methodists reflected the presence of the Holy Spirit in their lives. Their joy was irrepressible. They were people of great vigor, zeal, enthusiasm, and exuberance; and this spirit carried over to their church services, which were punctuated with rousing outbursts of "Hallelujah," loud "Amens," and glad cries of "Glory to God, Praise the Lord." Suffice to say you don't find that sort of "carryings on" in The Methodist Church today—or in any other "orthodox" denominational gathering. A woman told me not long ago that many people go to a particular Methodist church in Nashville, Tennessee, to hear a strange old man say "Amen" out loud.

The reason the early Methodists were so full of joy was that they had the assurance that no matter how scarlet were their past sins, because of Christ they were washed as white as snow. A drunkard just off the streets, having received the witness of the Spirit, could say with Paul, "Christ Jesus came into the world to save sinners; of whom I am chief" (I Tim. 1:15, KJV).

The Holy Spirit is available to everyone, preached Wesley, and you don't need a theological education to begin proclaiming the good news that God was in Christ and is available now through the power of the Holy Spirit. There was a tremendous attractiveness about this dynamic new movement, and out of it came an army of lay preachers and class leaders who witnessed for the Spirit across the world. It was in the lives of these early Methodists and other Christian church people that the gospel message was proven true, as they became aware by the grace of God that there was an infinite good creatively working in their lives.

I have reached the conclusion that the blasphemy against the Holy Spirit which will not be forgiven occurs when man persists in thinking of himself as anything less than the temple of the Holy Spirit. That we should inwardly consider ourselves unworthy must be the subtlest of all the temptations Satan puts before us. God made us to have communion with him; in his own image he shaped us; and by his grace we may receive his Holy

Spirit. The conditions of God's good giving have nothing to do with our worthiness or unworthiness; rather it is a matter of our receptivity, and God trusts that we shall choose to receive.

A story is told concerning one of England's most gifted preachers. As a boy he had the reputation of being an unruly scoundrel. His parents were convinced that he was incorrigible and would never amount to anything. Late one night he came home drunk and with shoes in hand began to climb the staircase leading up to his room. A door opened at the top of the stairs, and all at once his grandmother stood before him carrying a lighted candle, the light of which wreathed her beautiful face. She looked like an angel. Then she put her hand on his shoulder and spoke five words that changed his life: "John, I believe in you." With head in hands he sobbed his heart out and prayed that God would save him.

All through this chapter I have been trying to tell you who you are and what belongs to you. By the power of the Holy Spirit, everything is yours—and you belong to Christ, and Christ belongs to God.

As the marsh-hen secretly builds on the watery sod,
Behold I will build me a nest on the greatness of God:
I will fly in the greatness of God as the marsh-hen flies
In the freedom that fills all the space 'twixt the marsh and
  skies:
By so many roots as the marsh-grass sends in the sod
I will heartily lay me a-hold on the greatness of God:
Oh, like to the greatness of God is the greatness within
The range of the marshes, the liberal marshes of Glynn.

2
The Ministries

The Ecumenical question is primarily a question of the Holy Spirit.

—James McCord

Paul was a genius at putting things in their proper perspective. To those contending factions in the Corinthian church, each claiming to follow Paul or Apollos or Cephas, the great apostle said, "All things are yours, whether Paul or Apollos or Cephas" (I Cor. 3:21-22).

I am fully persuaded of the serious problems that lie at the very heart of modern church life. Our resources are so abundant, our opportunities are so great, and yet our triumphs are comparatively few. Many churchmen believe that our impotence is the direct result of our denominational divisions. They say that if we could just unite the dissected body of Christ, we would have the strength of organic oneness. In this chapter we shall discuss the pros and cons of church union in light of the Holy Spirit's guidance.

All the ministries of Jesus Christ belong to us when we are in Christ. There is a powerful word here for the modern church. Perhaps somewhere between the idea of one organic church union and the continuing Protestant pluralism, which Lloyd J. Averill has called "a legitimate Christian compulsion to a certain organic separateness," an amplified meaning of "everything is yours" should be heard.

Several years ago a church congregation in my community split on the issue of how the Holy Spirit manifests himself. Approximately half the congregation resigned their membership and proceeded to purchase a plot of ground adjoining the property of their former church home. Within a few months the dissenters had constructed a building, hired a preacher, and were conducting worship services under a new denominational name. The sad result of this peevish schism has been the gradual deterioration in the life of both churches.

Church congregations that separate for no better reason than incompatibility are the open sore of modern Protestantism. The most ridiculous story on congregational disputes that has come to my attention was one about a church that divided on the gripping issue of whether to seed or sod the church yard.

As a Protestant I do not take pride in the fact that many Protestant denominations and individual church groups have indulged themselves in radical disputes, resulting in the establishment of some 267 denominations in America. However, I am proud to say that we are inheritors of the Reformation principle of creative dissent, and within the framework of such a legacy there are bound to be outcroppings of a sometimes inordinate individualism. I am not for one moment upholding the wild-eyed, "we have the only truth" cults whose bizarre idiosyncrasies have damaged, rather than helped, the cause of Christ. But still there is more to be said for a variety of worship expressions, through which I can exercise my Protestant option, than to have my freedom in worship opportunities limited by the amalgamation of the various churches into one superchurch.

There are several strong arguments set forth by those who have an "urge to merge" into a unified church. First, the powerful influence of the Roman Catholic Church in high places speaks well for the sort of concentrated authority that can command power and exercise it through the application of pressure when the need exists. The Protestant churches have a limited influence because of their separateness. Second, the ever dangerous world situation challenges Protestant churches to speak with a singleness of faith and purpose, so that it may be heard when decisions are being made that affect the future of mankind. The divided church has a limited range of effective transmission. Third, by consolidating the scattered forces of the church, a well-organized, highly efficient, heavily financed, organic Protestant church could create a Christian culture and subdue the beleaguering secular forces in our society. Fourth, an ecumenical church can minister more effectively in the mission field because it presents one message and one approach to the Christian life. The pooled resources of several churches would hasten the conversion of many lands. Fifth, Jesus prayed "that they [interpreted as the church] may all be one; even as thou, Father, art in me, and I in thee, that they also may be in us, so that the world may believe that thou hast sent me" (John 17:21). And as Paul says in Ephesians, "There is one body and one Spirit, just as you were called to the one hope that belongs to your call, one Lord, one faith, one baptism, one God and Father of us all, who is above all and through all and in all" (Eph. 4:4-6).

On the other side of the discussion there is an equally strong opinion on this matter of artificial church merger. The opposition voice, which includes my own, will tell you first of all that human nature being what it is presupposes an eventual authoritarian administration and rule that would rob Protestantism of the freedom it has struggled through the centuries to advance and maintain. Could the superchurch escape "a heavy-handed hierarchy of a few chairborne soldiers bossing the whole army"? As one of my friends is fond of saying, "I wouldn't mind having a hierarchy if I could be the head of it."

Second, church union thinking is analogous to that of big business and big unions, where extensive mergers create more capital, close out competition, improve efficiency, eliminate waste, and gain more power for effective administration. Must the church emulate the economic patterns of the power-crazed culture in which we live? Is the organic church union dream more of human than divine design?

Third, in this day of mass movements, when monolithic bigness is worshiped as a God, are we not, even in a free society, in danger of losing the chief necessity of freedom —namely, a variety of choices by which we may exercise our freedom to choose? If Methodists, Presbyterians, Episcopalians, and members of the United Church of Christ were suddenly swept into one homogeneous organization, as Eugene Carson Blake has suggested in his

31

proposal for church union, then I could no longer choose to be distinctively Methodist or Presbyterian or Episcopalian or United Church, because my choices would have been eliminated. I believe that modern democratic man does not need more freedom. He needs instead a greater opportunity to use the freedom he has. Let the churches, by remaining structurally separate, protect what few opportunities we have left to practice our freedom.

Consider, as the fourth point, if you will, the amount of administrative machinery that would be required to hold together such diverse denominational emphases and doctrinal beliefs as: the Trinitarian and Unitarian theological formulas; virgin birth; pre-existence of Christ; mystical Christ; historical Jesus; Christ's bodily resurrection; Christ's resurrection influence; the Word of God as a human record; the Word of God as divinely infallible; the second coming of Christ; the definition of the sacraments; and the kind of government which is best able to administrate the church—Presbyterian, Episcopalian, or Congregational. Can all of these be held together by a single interpretation of John 17:21? How could the leadership of this organic church union escape the peril of power which portends to the multiplication of man's machinery and a diminution of God's power?

The emphases that give Protestantism its pluralistic image are not academic; though unfortunately few Protestants know exactly what their denominations do emphasize. Systems of thought and belief have, in many instances, come into being by a fiery ordeal and tremendous sacrifice. If anyone is naïve enough to suppose that theological differences are just superficial bric-a-brac that can be disposed of by an ecumenical committee or council, then let him give closer examination to post-Reformation church history. There are some stubborn Protestants unwilling to give up an entire denominational heritage for the purpose of speaking with one voice and by one interpretation of John 17:21. If the deep desire of the ecumenical advocate is for a single voice with which to confess his faith, can he not hear the wearisome Roman Catholic invitation to the separated Protestant brethren—"We're waiting"? The questions that must be answered by the exponents of church union are: Who will speak for us; what will he say; and at what cost?

Those of us who are "holding out" against major church merger, for fear of seeing the church enveloped in a colorless fog of uniformity, are being told that the organized church union would "protect" the tradition of Protestant denominations by establishing a system of orders similar to the structure of the Roman Catholic Church. This "breath-taking vision," as one merger-minded man has termed it, visualizes our Protestant denominations becoming like the Franciscan, Dominican, or Jesuit Orders of the Roman Catholic Church, who relinquish something to the mother church but retain certain theoretical differences for a purely conventional value. Evidently the "something" given up is the right of dissent and freedom of choice. I submit that this is too great a price in exchange for a handful of philosophical orders that exist for conventional value. The acid test for the merger enthusiast, simply put, is how much of his church freedom is he willing to surrender?

The very expression "ecumenical" is bandied about by

many people with only the vaguest understanding of what it means. I cannot accept the definition of the ecumenical movement as a syncretism (merger of several into one) of all the major denominations into one established organized church. Ecumenics has to do with a continuing dialogue between the separate churches and the sharing of those experiences that bring greater awareness of our oneness with Christ. I believe in the ecumenical movement as a means of affirming the oneness that separate churches share in the Body of Christ, while holding to their functional diversity within the Body.

For just as the body is one and has many members, and all the members of the body, though many, are one body, so it is with Christ. (I Cor. 12:12.)

For the body does not consist of one member but of many. If the foot should say, "Because I am not a hand, I do not belong to the body," that would not make it any less a part of the body. And if the ear should say, "Because I am not an eye, I do not belong to the body," that would not make it any less a part of the body. If the whole body were an eye, where would be the hearing? If the whole body were an ear, where would be the sense of smell? But as it is, God arranged the organs in the body, each one of them, as he chose. (I Cor. 12:14-18.)

But still there is a foot, a hand, an eye, and an ear, representing the separate units within the unity of the body. Daniel Day Williams has said a word that seems appropriate to repeat here.

It is even necessary to see that the work of the Holy Spirit may create new divisions among men. Christ asserted a new perspective upon life against others. So we may understand the saying about his bringing not peace but a sword. Men have some of their profoundest disagreements over what the Lord requires of them. Consider the divisions among the Christian churches. The Spirit does not blot out such divisions, though in The Spirit we are required to search for the misunderstandings and the sins which are in them. The Holy Spirit will be found where we learn to live in creative conflict, respecting one another's humanity and faith even where we have profound differences over fundamental issues.[1]

Searching for a contemporary application of Paul's words, "all things are yours, whether Paul or Apollos or Cephas," I would like to think that all the truth of God's Word, pronounced through the various churches, belongs to me because of Christ. Is it not an admission of spiritual failure when we attempt to consolidate the visible church because we cannot or will not apprehend what is already established invisibly? The greatest challenge to the twentieth-century churchman is that he come into relationship with the living Christ and by the power of the Holy Spirit lead his separate church into a great spiritual renewal. The world is not waiting for the emergence of a superchurch, but rather for a powerful witness of Christ's presence within the existing churches, that will draw them into a spiritual unity of one body, one Spirit, one hope, one Lord, one faith, and one baptism in the Holy Spirit. J. B. Phillips translates Paul this way:

[1] *The Minister and the Care of Souls* (New York: Harper & Row, 1961), p. 131.

Make it your aim to be at one in the Spirit, and you will inevitably be at peace with one another. You all belong to one body, of which there is one Spirit, just as you all experienced one calling to one hope. There is one Lord, one faith, one baptism, one God, one Father of us all, who is the one over all, the one working through all and the one living in all. (Eph. 4:3-6).

The unity we should seek is the unity that seeks us by the power of the Holy Spirit, causing us to become aware of the oneness we already possess in the Body of Christ.

It seems to me that visible church union by its very nature would tend to ignore the Spirit's diversity, through which new wine may be poured into new wineskins and without which there is only deadly stagnation. I am convinced that organizational church union will not increase the vitality of the merging churches. Man's attempt to artificially construct such a union falls under the judgment of God's Word, "Not by might nor by power, but by my Spirit, says the Lord of hosts" (Zech. 4:6).

In his inimitable manner, Peter DeVries humorously pictures the chancel area of a church that has attempted to theologically blend the unblendable and harmonize that which cannot be harmonized.

There is a small worship area at one end. This has a platform cantilevered on both sides, with a free-form pulpit designed by Noguchi. It consists of a slab of marble set on four legs of four delicately different fruitwoods, to symbolize the four Gospels, and their failure to harmonize. Behind it dangles a large multicolored mobile, its interdenominational parts swaying, as one might fancy, in perpetual reminder of the Pauline stricture against those "blown by every wind of doctrine." [2]

Many glowing accounts have been written concerning the merger of the churches in South India and the great work that has been accomplished through this ecumenical advance. However, Gerald Kennedy has written, "I must report that one of its [the Church of South India] leaders told me in confidence that he could not honestly say there was more vitality or effectiveness in its life than had been manifested in the separate bodies which formed it." [3]

When I consider how much I owe the various churches, with their peculiar emphases that have fed my soul from time to time, I feel a ghostly chill at the thought that something of this would be lost in the creation of a single organized church.

The church in which I have membership has long been called a "melting pot" denomination, because it does not have a specific doctrinal standard to which all must pledge allegiance in order to become a member.

The spirit of John Wesley pervades the life of this denomination from worship and song to prayer and polity. If there is one great idea around which the church rallies, it is the experience of a "warmed heart." The deep spiritual experience of John Wesley on May 24, 1738, at a meetinghouse on Aldersgate Street in London launched

[2] *The Mackeral Plaza* (Boston: Little, Brown and Company, 1958), p. 7.

[3] *The Challenge to Reunion,* ed. Robert A. Brown and David H. Scott (New York: McGraw-Hill, 1963), p. 225.

what has become a world-wide movement. Wesley once commented, "I look upon all the world as my parish." An analogous comment today might be construed as denominational imperialism.

Distinctive ideas of Methodism are: (1) the witness of the Holy Spirit in a person's life; (2) regeneration as the proven way to finding salvation in God; (3) and the teaching that it is possible to become perfect in love in this life. I like to think that all of this belongs to me, not just because I am a Methodist, but because of Christ.

The Presbyterian church, through a high-school youth group, introduced me to certain life-changing emphases that helped immeasurably during my teen-age years. The Presbyterians taught me about: (1) the sovereignty of God in Christ in the salvation of each person; (2) each believer's salvation is a part of a divine plan; (3) salvation is a spiritual gift from God and is not a reward for faith; (4) man cannot save himself; (5) regeneration is the work of God alone; and (6) those who are once saved will always remain saved.

Because of Christ all of this belongs to me even though I am not a member of the Presbyterian Church. At a crucial moment in my life, the Calvinistic theological formula gave me insight into the eternal plan of God which translated itself into terms that I could understand.

The Lutheran Church ministered to me through part of my college life. The life of Martin Luther was so real that when I made my first visit to Rome I went directly to the Lateran Church in front of which is the famed *Scala Sancta,* the twenty-eight-step staircase, supposedly the actual flight of stairs leading up to the palace of Pontius Pilate. On my hands and knees I climbed each step, just as Luther once did, saying a prayer on each, and finally declaring at the summit, as did Luther, "Who knows whether it is so!"

One day while in seminary I drew a picture of Luther's face, using an old woodcut as my guide. With each stroke of the charcoal I became more impressed by the courage and determination in this man's countenance. There was another characteristic there too, but I wasn't sure of what it was until I had finished the drawing; then I saw it as the feature that made the face so masterful—it was the likeness of impregnable faith.

Many times Protestants, when confronted by a time of crisis, have read an account of the events that occurred on that memorable afternoon of April 17, 1521, when Martin Luther appeared before the Diet of Worms. Luther had become a national hero to the German people, but on this day he would face the emperor of the Holy Roman Empire, Charles V, to answer charges of heresy. Luther stood beside a table on which were piled several books that he had authored. These books were written protests against the sale of indulgences (a guarantee of free passage through purgatory into heaven) for the pope's building program in the Vatican. Luther was given twenty-four hours to decide if he would recant the message in the books.

On the next day in the great hall, filled with smoke from the many torches, Luther made his formal reply before a large assembly:

39

If his Imperial Majesty desires a plain answer, I will give him one without horns and without teeth, and it is this: It is impossible for me to recant unless I am proved to be in the wrong by the testimony of the Scriptures or by evident reasoning; I cannot trust either the decisions of Councils or Popes, for it is plain that they have not only erred, but have contradicted each other. My conscience is chained to the word of God, and it is neither safe nor honest to act against one's conscience. God help me!

The emperor interrupted—the hall was astir—Luther spoke again, "Here I stand, I cannot do otherwise." That moment belongs to every Protestant Christian.

My Lutheran friends helped me see the meaning of: (1) justification by faith alone. Luther added the word "alone" in the margin of the scriptural page; (2) the word of God is the only rule of faith; (3) the Lord's Supper is a channel of God's grace; and (4) baptism is the threshold into regeneration for the Holy Spirit.

Because of Christ all of this belongs to me, though I am not a member of the Lutheran Church.

Some of my highest moments in prayer and meditation have come in Roman Catholic churches and chapels which, unlike their Protestant counterparts, are always open day or night. There are few times that I pass without entering a lovely chapel in one of the great Roman Catholic hospitals in our city. In that place I have felt the presence of the Holy Spirit. I have always been impressed by the way the Roman Catholic Masses are scheduled to meet the needs of the worshiping people. High Mass is celebrated at 10:00 A.M. and noon on Sundays, and a sermon is delivered. Low Mass is celebrated from 5:00 A.M. until 10:00 A.M. on Sundays. Vespers are sung on Sunday afternoon or evening. A Mass is said daily by the priest. Special services are held on Friday and on all holy days. There is a flexibility about the time schedule for daily services to make them available to the largest number of people.

Though I find little in Roman Catholicism with which I completely agree, I still admire the individual Catholic's devotion to his church and his church's apparent interest in providing people all over the world with open chapels and churches in which to worship God. Because of Christ, the Roman Catholic Church belongs to me because I have prayed in it and have found God there.

Each summer when vacationing on the Gulf Coast, I worship on Sunday mornings in a lovely Baptist church. There is no church in the world that loves liberty more than the Baptist, and this independent spirit is abundantly evident in each Baptist church that I have visited. I have been thrilled by the emphasis on tithing and evangelism so obviously important to the Baptist people. They continually sound the alarm to warn other American Protestant churches concerning any encroachments on our cherished blessing of the separation between church and state. Their emphasis on baptism by immersion has deeply impressed me, and perhaps after all is said and done we must admit that their way is the appropriate manner. The world is indebted to the tithing Baptists who are able to underwrite great missionary projects and extend the influence of Christ. Because of Christ the Baptist

41

church belongs to me, though I am not one of their members.

The Protestant Episcopal Church has never let me forget for a moment how beautiful worship can and should be. I will not soon forget the experience of listening to a young priest explain the architectural design of his church. "Out there," he said, letting his hand move across the congregational area of the nave, "is the Church Militant—the center aisle ascends slightly as you walk from the foyer to the front of the sanctuary. The chancel area is the Church Expectant—here we commune, and overhead you will notice the cross." A huge cross was suspended over the Communion rail. "We come by way of the cross to the place of expectation. The area up where the high altar is, we call the Church Triumphant! There the elements of Christ's presence are blessed."

I have worshiped and led worship in several Episcopal churches, and in each instance the beauty of the liturgy, the glorious music, the lovely architecture, and above all the Spirit of Christ's brooding presence, have combined to insure a memorable spiritual experience. Because of Christ the Episcopal Church belongs to me, although I am not a member of it.

The Quakers, or Religious Society of Friends, are responsible for giving me an introduction to the value of silence in worship. My initial experience with the "First Day" meeting was at Earlham College in an old meetinghouse. These Quaker meetinghouses are plain and unadorned. The Quaker Friends have no creeds or sacraments. They refuse to take an oath, and they will not fight. They simply cultivate the experience of God. They believe in a baptism of the Spirit and fellowship with the Father and Son as the fulfillment of their spiritual life. Because of Christ they belong to me, though I am not a member of their Society.

The Swedenborgian, or Church of the New Jerusalem, introduced me to the spiritual giant Emanuel Swedenborg. One cold winter's day I enjoyed a pleasant conversation with a pastor of this church before an open fire in his church library. He succeeded in whetting my appetite to read some of the important writings of Swedenborg.

Emanuel Swedenborg was one of the most celebrated scientists of the early eighteenth century. He was honored many times by the crowned heads of Europe for his scientific achievements. Then, at the height of his brilliant career, he entered into constant contact with the spiritual world, retaining and exercising all his normal powers of observation and reflection. He was able to step from this world to the next, converse with the spiritual beings, then return to faithfully, analytically, and systematically record, as a good scientist would, his experiences. The world acclaimed him again as a person with unprecedented psychic power.

Anyone who reads Swedenborg is impressed by his absolute sincerity and intellectual powers. His writings are not those of a madman, but of a seer with a profound witness.

Helen Keller wrote, "Whatever may be the opinion of those who read Swedenborg's religious books, one cannot but be impressed by his unique personality. He did everything gently and deliberately. There was nothing of excitement or elation about him. The farther he traveled in

43

the spiritual realm, the more humble and composed he became." [4]

After reading some of Swedenborg's writings, I have come to the conclusion that if heaven is as he pictured it, then we may look forward to all that is there with exciting anticipation. Helen Keller says of Swedenborg, "Heaven unbarred to him her lofty gates." The Swedenborgian Church is a movement rather than a sect. Swedenborgians worship in churches of many denominations. Swedenborg's vision for the church was one in which men of all faiths and creeds would find their spiritual likeness in spiritual union rather than sectarian unity. Swedenborg dreamed of a united Christianity based on spiritual accord. The Church of the New Jerusalem is directed toward this end. I am not a member of the Swedenborg Church, but because of Christ I feel it belongs to me.

The Pentecostal Church has ministered to me with its emphasis on holiness and sanctification. Pentecostal evangelistic enthusiasm and exciting worship services are emotionally satisfying and deeply stirring. I have learned from these people the meaning of the scriptural verse:

Keep your heart with all vigilance;
for from it flow the springs of life (Prov. 4:23).

The Pentecostal seeks to release the flow of the Holy Spirit's power through his life as a witness of the Spirit's presence, and should the rational sense be offended by any manifestation of this power then it must be put aside. The

[4] Helen Keller, *My Religion* (New York: Swedenborg Foundation Inc., 1945), p. 24.

baptism of the Holy Spirit, evincing itself through the gift of speaking in tongues, is accepted by the Pentecostal people as a height in spiritual development, and I have no reason to quarrel with them. The Pentecostal Church is a powerful instrument of the Lord, and because of Christ I feel a part of it, though I am not a member. James McCord referred to the Pentecostals in his address to the students and faculty at the opening of a semester at Princeton Theological Seminary:

The Ecumenical question is primarily a question of the Holy Spirit. Are we willing as a church among churches to let the Holy Spirit be responsible for the churches' life? . . . It is disturbing that the World Council of Churches has not dealt with this question as a major theme in any general council, nonetheless it is precisely because our own institutions are at stake, that ours must become the age of the Spirit of God active in the world shaking and shattering all our forms and structures and bringing forth responses consonant with the Gospel and the world need. This is why in our own age the Pentecostals have begun to attract the attention of classical Protestantism. They have been able to move into countries with a flexibility we do not possess and through their ministry produce the fruit of the Spirit in the lives of men. Brethren, when we began to program we lose the flexibility that the Holy Spirit gives. We who have stifled the fire of the Spirit of God now see it blazing up in other groups as judgment upon us. God's spirit refuses to be stifled even by the church. No, especially not by the church, because judgment begins in the house of the Lord!

Dr. McCord brings us back to the question of what the Holy Spirit wants the church to do in our day. I believe

45

that any proposal for unification of the visible church is an admission that the separate churches are weak and unable to provide the necessary Christian witness so desperately needed in our times. The uniting of several weak churches does not mean that a strong church will emerge. What we may have is a weak unified church.

Dedicated and devoted merger enthusiasts are conscientiously trying to organize the church. I do not doubt their sincerity nor their intent, but it seems rather presumptuous that they venture so far in planning for unifying the body of Christ visibly without caring for the ills of their own local or denominational churches. Merger-minded Christians need to face the unpleasant contemporary fact that many churches, perhaps their own, are spiritually sick, and it seems improbable that by merely gathering the separate ailing churches behind one banner, under one roof, and around one Communion table that a cure will be found for the epidemic. If anything, the infection will be spread.

Most people enjoy being swept along on the tide of the exciting and spectacular, and certainly church people are as vulnerable to this inclination as anyone else. For instance, if those who are so obsessed with the idea of a big church union were to quietly roll up their sleeves and channel their considerable energies in getting on with the less glamorous, but vastly more important, task of developing within their separate churches a spiritual life movement, a new spiritual revival would break out that would shake the foundations of the earth. I am convinced that Christians need to be taught how to pray, how to read the Bible, how to receive the Holy Spirit, and how to witness; but someone must lead them. Since no Christian is sufficient to himself, he needs to be yoked with others who share a common need of guidance and goal. It is within the context of a spiritual life group movement that revival begins, but someone must lead forth by putting "first things first." Members of the spiritual life groups in our church are so filled with the Holy Spirit that they are leading a great spiritual awakening across our city. But revival does not begin until people are baptized in the Holy Spirit. Jesus did not preach a single sermon until he was baptized with the Spirit.

Jesus urged his followers to pray for the Holy Spirit. He said, "If you then, who are evil, know how to give good gifts to your children, how much more will the heavenly Father give the Holy Spirit to those who ask him?" (Luke 11:13.)

Jesus is suggesting that his followers need the blessing of the Holy Spirit. Without the Holy Spirit there is no divine life, no deep sense of the presence of Jesus Christ, no growth in grace, no effective service, and no oneness with the Father. Let the people of God in the denominations pray to receive the Holy Spirit; who will reveal the spiritual union that already exists in the Body of Christ, that lives and moves and has its being through the variety of church expressions of the same truth.

It is easier to call a conference, convocation, or assembly for working out procedures and systems on how we shall unite the churches than to pray fervently, frequently, and believingly for the Holy Spirit to come and lead us.

47

Political maneuvering, theological debates, intellectual gymnastics, grandiose programs may someday succeed in stitching together part of what many people erroneously call the "Broken Body of Christ," the dismemberment and disunity of his body, sectarian fragmentation of the Christian fellowship, and scandalous apostate denominational system—to name a few choice epithets found in ecumenical literature. Such enormous effort would be more profitably exercised by coming to grips with the spiritual unity that already exists through the multidimensional Body of the living Christ. Since the Body of Christ is essentially spiritual and cannot be broken from without, it seems rather ludicrous that men should dedicate themselves so unstintingly to the gigantic task of trying to pull it together externally.

The oneness we seek will only come on the wings of spiritual apprehension of what already is. Perhaps all Christians should be at the task of praying for eyes to see the one true church—"a house not made with hands."

Must we go on year after year depending on man's wisdom, man's perception, man's experience, and man's energy to make the church vital and relevant. Can any human influence, including church merger, penetrate the heart of the church, burn its egocentricity, melt its prejudice, consume its pride, purge its sin, refine its life, except the fire of God that fell on Pentecost?

Church organization may merge or divide, increase or decrease, but nothing of spiritual significance will happen to the man in the church until that day Pentecost comes upon him. The whole church of God needs this experience and needs it desperately; she needs the upper room, the tarrying at Jerusalem, the power of the Holy Spirit, and a continuing Pentecost. Nothing less than this will give the church redemptive power equal to the challenge of a sin-sick world.

Co-operation among all the churches of Christ, dialogue between the denominations, and fellowship of common concern within the councils of churches are all important and worthwhile enterprises, but what church councils, denominations, and churches need most is to receive the promise of Jesus. "You shall receive power when the Holy Spirit has come upon you." (Acts 1:8.)

Receiving the Holy Spirit will inspire the individual Christian to witness in whatever place he is called to live and work. A mother will be anointed to train her family for service to the Lord. A Sunday-school teacher will be empowered to lead his class to a new relationship in Jesus Christ. The Holy Spirit will enable a church member to offer greater service to his church. When pastors are baptized in the Holy Spirit they will preach and lead with tremendous new power, and when the churches receive this blessing of God they shall discover what is meant by "oneness in the spirit" and "an army with banners."

The best evidence of a genuine spiritual hunger within all the churches is seen in the development of the spiritual life group movement, which is springing up like wildfire in all denominations of the Christian church.

In my church we have seen this movement grow until now we have fourteen of these groups, men, women, couples, youth, and mixed groups, meeting regularly at a variety of times and places throughout the week. The people in this "Yokefellow" movement (Common Discipline-Group Experience) have become aware of the holy power that holds them together and the presence of Christ in their midst. No wonder this movement is leaping denominational walls and church people are discovering their oneness in Christ. Members of the Yokefellow groups hold the following rule of life: (1) Daily prayer, alone and with the family; (2) daily scriptures, a short passage read slowly and reverently at the same time every day; (3) Christian fellowship, regular participation in both public worship and small group meetings; (4) proportionate giving, a definite portion of both money and time, joyously given to the Christian cause; (5) witness, unapologetic witness for Christ by use of the Yoke pin or in some other way, particularly in daily work; and (6) study, development of intellectual integrity by careful study of Christian books.

How thrilling it is to behold the denominational barriers, that have so long separated the people of God, coming down or at least being moved, not by what man is doing but because of the Holy Spirit.

There is a story told of a group of American soldiers who were quartered in a little French village and who became very friendly with all the villagers. One day the soldiers were called into action, and that night returned carrying one boy who would go to rest in the soil of France. The villagers went immediately to their priest and requested that the soldier be buried in their consecrated ground. The priest reluctantly refused because, though he was a fine brave boy, he was not of their faith. So he was buried as close to the cemetery wall as possible so that he would be near the beloved dead of the village.

The next day, to the joy and wonder of this entire community, the village folk discovered the boy's grave within the cemetery wall. During the night the old priest had moved the wall. Through this spiritual life renewal the churches' walls are being moved and people are literally experiencing a new birth and a new life.

Recently a sales executive in our church, whose territory covers one fourth of the United States, was telling me that everywhere he goes in his work he finds churchmen seeking to find some way of renewing the life within their own churches. They have a holy longing. These people do not want a formula—they want the Christ and the fulfilling of this word, "Blessed are they that hunger and thirst after righteousness, for they shall be filled" (Matt. 5:6).

Jesus prayed that the church be one, but the oneness for which he prayed can come only when people of all denominations receive his Holy Spirit and become conscious of his spiritual Body. Jesus did not pray for organizational uniformity, superchurch power bloc, or denominational merger. The unity Jesus prayed for was spiritual. Paul speaks to this point: "Till we all come in the unity of the faith, and of the knowledge of the Son of God, unto a perfect man, unto the measure of the stature of fulness of Christ" (Eph. 4:13, KJV).

This further points up the idea that the roadblocks to church unity are not organizational difference and doctrinal dispute, but rather the absence of a spiritual perception among the people of God. The road to real Christian unity leads by way of "faith and knowledge of the

Son of God" and learning to see with "the eyes of invisibles" the glorious vision of the Body of Christ.

Let us dedicate ourselves to the task of strengthening the ties that already exist within the visible church; not by mutual back scratching, but through dialogue and unification in various projects when we are led by God into these cooperative efforts. Let us cease holding the silly notion that the more we merge our denominations the stronger the Christian church will be—as though God needs our assistance in holding his Body together. Let us not be theologically browbeaten into compromising an iota of spiritual freedom or denominational emphasis because we are afraid of being branded "uncooperative" by the merger-minded brethren. Let us not forget nor forsake the diversity of our spiritual expression which gives zest and vitality to our Protestant churches. Let the denominational churches, with their peculiar ministries, keep their traditional personalities separate and distinct, but at the same time let us recognize that in Christ we already belong to one another. Then we will understand the meaning of Paul's words, "All things are yours, whether Paul or Apollos or Cephas."

3

The World

Is our world headed for destruction, or can it be saved?
Perhaps God has not yet made up His mind; perhaps He lets
our actions decide, perhaps His plan is to let us make up
our minds. This is what He does with individuals.

—Frank C. Laubach

"All things are yours, whether Paul or Apollos or
Cephas or the world . . . and you are Christ's, and Christ
is God's." Paul is pleading with us to see that, because of
our relationship to Christ, we are to overcome the world
and not be overcome by it. We are to assume redemptive
leadership of the world in the name and nature of our
Lord. The basic question is, How can we do this?

Because of Christ, we have a sovereignty over the
world. This does not mean that we shall receive a holy
exemption from the painful storms and stresses of life;
but with his presence in our lives we receive the power of
a divine checkmate as pain gives way to comfort, anguish
gives way to serenity, loneliness gives way to communion,
and storms give way to calm. In Christ we have the final
interpreter and translator of all our experience in the
world. It is he who defines the true meaning of life, and
through the Holy Spirit he gives us the authority to minister to the world.

53

Each Sunday morning I preach to my congregation facing a great balcony window that spells out the Christian's marching orders: "Go therefore and make disciples of all nations, baptizing them in the name of the Father and of the Son and of the Holy Spirit . . . and lo, I am with you always" (Matt. 28:19, 20). As Christians we cannot escape our responsibility to the world. We are members of the worldwide family of mankind in the household of God, therefore all human experience, no matter how far removed, somehow has a relationship to each of us. However, most of us would prefer to walk through this world with an averted gaze, maintaining a stoic detachment that would protect us from the pain of beholding the tragic condition of our brethren in distress; but as Christians we cannot afford such privileged immunity. At times we would like to cancel our membership in the family of man; regretfully lament that the world belongs to the devil; and simply adjust ourselves to the facts of life, cautiously hoping against hope and never being too optimistic about the future.

A Harvard professor, trying to find a philosophy for living in his troubled times, was asked, "If you could write a history of the world, how many books would it fill?" He replied:

I could do it in ten volumes; no—perhaps five volumes; no . . . I could write it in a booklet; no—it could be published in an essay; no—it could be condensed to a pamphlet; no—I could write it in one sentence, "The mills of the Gods grind slowly and they grind exceedingly small, the honey bee

54

pollinates the flower it robs and when the night gets dark enough the stars come out!"

This highly symbolic and beautiful bit of prose stands pale and wanting beside the revelation of God's philosophy concerning the world: "God so loved the world that he gave his only Son" (John 3:16).

The living Christ leads us away from a stoic or pessimistic way of thinking concerning our life and the world. We need to affirm the fact that the world does not belong to Satan, but rather to God. The Holy Spirit of God speaking through Paul plainly announces, "All things are yours."

In the days of his flesh this extraordinary comment was made concerning him: "He taught them as one who had authority, and not as the scribes" (Mark 1:22). Interestingly, the scribes did have authority. They were among the religious authorities of their day, but Jesus possessed a higher authority. You may tell me what the Bible says; how a creed reads; what you have read in a recent book on religion; or what the bishop's views are on a particular subject; and I may or may not accept your authority. I have often witnessed people attempting to persuade others to accept a particular point of view concerning the Christian faith and succeeding only in evoking hostility and defensiveness in their listeners. This has led me to consider the difference between expressing a point of view and speaking with authority.

Jesus spoke with authority, not as the scribes. He often said harsh things to people; he told men the truth about themselves, yet they listened and followed him in

55

ever increasing numbers. What was his secret? Certainly it must become ours if we are to serve our Lord effectively. The Greek word for authority is *exousia,* which is best defined, "out of that which is one's very own." Jesus Christ spoke out of that which belonged to him. His authority was deeply rooted in the reality of his spiritual union with the Father. This is where *our* authority must be anchored.

We have had the experience of hearing hundreds of people talk about the Christian faith, and at times these people seem to be saying, in a general way, the same thing. But listening more intently, we discover it is not so much what they were saying but rather the authentic or nonauthentic way in which their faith was stated. If you listen closely you can recognize the difference between the secondhand witness for Christ and the sort of word that comes out of experiences in the deep recesses of a person's communion with the Holy Spirit. It is the authority of Christ, resident in our lives, that can effectively witness to the world and bring about its transformation.

A few weeks ago I was seated in the sanctuary of a lovely church, waiting my turn to address an assembly of churchwomen in their annual conference meeting. The devotional period preceding my talk was led by a young minister obviously crushed beneath the burden of troubling world events. His words were painfully pessimistic and tearfully hopeless. His despair was so contagious that I literally fought the impulse to lapse into melancholy.

At first I thought my gloomy mood was engendered by the heavy odor or aroma (depending on your point of view) of coffee. The women attending the conference had recently eaten their lunch in an assembly room beneath the sanctuary, and the pungent smell of the coffee was beginning to envelop the room in which we were meeting. At length I realized that it was not the coffee odor that was afflicting me but rather the despondent message, which grew so fretful that it sounded like a soulful dirge or an ancient taunt—a taunt resembling that found in the forty-second psalm, where the adversaries of the psalmist are needling him by constantly asking, "Where is your God?" "Where is thy God?"

It was then, by the power of the Holy Spirit, that I began to preach the gospel message to a congregation paralyzed with the bad news of the world. I would like to be on record as emphatically declaring that our world is not going to pieces, despite all the foreboding news concerning war and rumors of war. What are falling apart are some of the untenable notions with which we have been content to live; for example, that we can ignore the power of God and survive in this world filled with evil hosts that threaten to undo us. God alone can exorcise the demonic element so prevalent in the world.

As an American citizen I have tremendous love and loyalty for my government, and am certain that it is doing everything within its power to protect and defend our democratic way of life and advance the cause of freedom around the world. But as a Christian I feel the compelling obligation to do what I can to help save the world through prayer, by preaching and teaching the lordship of Jesus Christ, by working for peace, and attempting to bring the world under the authority of God through the power of the Holy Spirit.

57

Wherever we consider the enemies of our way of life we automatically think of communism. It would be well for us to remember that communism is nothing more than an instrument of Satan. Yet we attempt to disguise this fact beneath a verbal facade of political and ecclesiastical sophistication. We need only to examine the rise and expansion of communism throughout the world to determine its origin. In 1917 Lenin led forty thousand dedicated Bolsheviks into what was then old Russia, and since that time communism has so extended its influence that today one third of the human race, or nearly a billion people, are behind communist boundaries. The dedication of the Communist to his godless religion is eloquently stated in a letter written by a young man from an eastern university to his fiancèe, breaking off their engagement after he had become a convert to communism while vacationing in Mexico. This letter was given to Billy Graham by a Presbyterian minister in Montreat, North Carolina. The young man wrote:

We Communists have a high casualty rate. We're the ones who get shot and hung and lynched and tarred and feathered and jailed and slandered and ridiculed and fired from our jobs, and in every other way made as uncomfortable as possible. A certain percentage of us get killed or imprisoned. We live in virtual poverty. We turn back to the party every penny we make above what is absolutely necessary to keep us alive. We Communists don't have the time or the money for many movies, or concerts, or T-bone steaks, or decent homes and new cars. We've been described as fanatics. We are fanatics. Our lives are dominated by one great over-shadowing factor—the struggle for world Communism. We

Communists have a philosophy of life which no amount of money could buy. We have a cause to fight for, a definite purpose in life. We subordinate our petty personal selves into a great movement of humanity, and if our personal lives seem hard, or our egos appear to suffer through subordination to the Party, then we are adequately compensated by the thought that each of us in his small way is contributing to something new and true and better for mankind. There is one thing in which I am in dead earnest and that is the Communist cause. It is my life, my business, my religion, my hobby, my sweetheart, my wife and mistress, my bread and meat, I work at it in the daytime and dream of it at night. Its hold on me grows, not lessens, as time goes on. Therefore I cannot carry on a friendship, a love affair or even a conversation without relating to this force which both drives and guides my life. I evaluate people, books, ideas and action according to how they affect the Communist cause and by their attitude toward it. I've already been in jail because of my ideas and, if necessary, I'm ready to go before a firing squad.[1]

The devotion and zeal of this young man are shared by millions in a world that is going Communist at the rate of 100 million per year, according to James Michener. Communism is a religion propelled by a spiritual force. It is a satanic religion motivated by evil power. Paul puts the matter before us in a succinct statement addressed to our times: "Put on the whole armor of God, that you may be able to stand against the wiles of the devil. For we are

[1] From a sermon by Dr. Graham, "Call to Commitment" (Minneapolis: The Billy Graham Evangelistic Association.) Used by permission.

not contending against flesh and blood, but against the principalities, against the powers, against the world rulers of this present darkness, against the spiritual hosts of wickedness in the heavenly places" (Eph. 6:11-12).

Let us discuss how we might set up a spiritual offensive against the communist advance. Certainly we will need to take up the chief weapons of our warfare in this spiritual struggle. If Christian people would become aware of the tremendous spiritual power at their disposal, we would enter a new era in world history. We give a name to each age representing the greatest power that man has been able to release. We have called this "the atomic age." By the power of God we might call the next world epoch "the spiritual age."

The power of prayer is virtually an untapped resource. Jesus said to his friends, "Truly, truly I say to you, he who believes in me will also do the works that I do; and greater works than these will he do, because I go to the Father. Whatever you ask in my name, I will do it, that the Father may be glorified in the Son; if you ask anything in my name, I will do it" (John 14:12-14).

It must be clearly understood that, though we may claim this gift of power by the promise of Christ, it still does not belong to us. This spiritual power is God-given in the name and nature of Jesus Christ through the gift of the Holy Spirit. Whoever thinks that he has God's power in and of himself deceives himself and is without power. We are not the voice, only the loudspeaker; we are not the music, only the instrument; we are not the power, only the medium. Therefore, we can accept no praise or glory for what has been given us by God; we ascribe all glory and honor to him.

First let us consider certain prevailing conditions for effective prayer. Among the first of these is the matter of surrendering our wills to the will of God and the emptying of ourselves. When self is too much involved in the process of our praying, then we block the channel of his creative living. It is not enough just to confess our sins; we need to be filled with the Holy Spirit. Often people who are utterly convicted of their sinfulness have emptied themselves in confession, but still do not prevail in prayer. We must pray to be filled with the Holy Spirit that he may use us effectively. Then his words become our words, his thoughts become our thoughts, and his energy flows through us. Indeed, we can say with the psalmist: "The Lord is the strength of my life" (Ps. 27:1, KJV). So powerful is this way of praying that even the forbidding mountains of this world, occupied by evil forces, will be cast down and overcome by the power of God.

We need to be disciplined in our praying. Plagued by the awful burden of civil war, Abraham Lincoln was in constant prayer during those terrible years. I am convinced that his emergence from that awful ordeal as perhaps the greatest president in our country's history was the direct result of his power in prayer. Not only did Mr. Lincoln attend church on Sunday morning at the New York Avenue Presbyterian Church, he was a regular attendant at midweek prayer meetings. He did not sit in the lecture room with the other people, but would seclude himself in the study of the pastor, Phineas Gurley. Usually his presence would go undetected because he would use a

61

side door to the church. However, sometimes on winter nights the people at the prayer meetings would recognize the huge Lincoln footprints in the snow.

We must not limit God in our praying. At the outset of World War II the entire British army was trapped in an indefensible position in Dunkirk on the coast of western Belgium. They seemed doomed to either capture or annihilation, in what surely would have been recorded as one of the most decisive military defeats in European history. The only possible escape route from the advancing Nazi army would have been across the sea, but at that time of the year such a crossing by boat or plane would be next to impossible due to heavy fog and turbulent waters.

The king of England, aware of the awful predicament, spoke on the radio to the people of Britain, beseeching them to go to their churches, repent of their sins, and pray that these men might be saved. It seemed an impossible task, but all across the country the church bells tolled and men, women, and children were called to repentance and prayer. What happened is all faithfully recorded in the history books under the intriguing caption, "The Miracle of Dunkirk."

One night a calm descended on the sea and the fog lifted for several hours, two events that have rarely if ever occurred in the history of recorded weather. A huge fleet of little boats were taken out of dry docks and put into the water, and along with hundreds of other rescue crafts under the protection of a thin screen of antiquated aircraft, they made their way to Dunkirk to rescue more than 335,000 British and French soldiers whom the Nazis had already counted upon as prisoners of war.

Some people might conclude that "the miracle at Dunkirk" was not a miracle at all but only a lucky happenstance or a fortunate turn of fate. Still others would call it an astounding miracle, tremble a bit, and cross themselves; but there are a few who might understand that the rescue of the men at Dunkirk had come about, not by chance nor the capricious imposition of divine will but rather by meeting the exacting conditions of a spiritual law. In the churches and homes of Britain people were repenting of their sins and claiming the divine gift.

We must come to understand that when we pray we simply launch out on the promises of Jesus. "Whatever you ask in my name, I will do it, that the Father may be glorified in the Son." (John 14:13.) We are not trying to remind God of his promises or coax him to fulfill his responsibilities to us. For example, when we pray for another person we should pray that the Holy Spirit will transmit the message in order to reach that person's subconscious mind. We should pray that the other person will listen to God and do his will. We are not telling anyone, including God, what to do; instead we are praying in the name and nature of Jesus Christ for others to receive the will of God for their lives and turn their minds toward his guidance. Perhaps what happened at Dunkirk could be explained scientifically, but someone needed to set in motion the events that transpired.

At Duke University J. B. Rhine is slowly but surely making believers of even the most antagonistic skeptics on the subject of thought transference. Most people at one time or another have had the experience of receiving a telepathic message from another person. We have discovered that distance is a relative factor in this kind of communication. The important considerations are the concentrated effort of the transmitter, the depth of the message, and the sensitivity of the hearer. I know a woman who generates such powerful transmission that nearly everyone, even with limited sensitivity, can receive her thoughts with very little effort.

During the time of the Cuban crisis in November, 1962, the United States and Soviet Union came perilously close to atomic war. Millions of Christians across the world were praying that this nuclear catastrophe would be averted. It is my belief that the prayers of all these people saved us from World War III. Some of these praying Christians were practicing directed prayer, which is a prayer method that follows closely the principle of thought transference, but by the power of the Holy Spirit goes deeper and is more powerful an instrument than any telepathic effort.

You may be wondering how it is possible to transmit a directed prayer to someone who might be asleep at the hour of your praying for him. Actually, this is the best time to send directed prayers to another person. While it is true that the conscious mind does sleep, it is equally true that the subconsicous mind never sleeps, and it is the subconscious mind—that nine tenths of our personality—that houses the great life-changing potential. However, the subconscious mind is subject to the conscious mind. The conscious mind, with its powerful censor and various mechanisms of defense, can reject both harmful and good ideas that might be suggested. In order to reach the subconscious mind at a time when reception of the good can take place, it would appear that the best time to pray a directive prayer for someone is after the person's conscious mind has gone to sleep. At that time the redemptive idea can be introduced into the subconscious mind.

This theory rests on practiced, reliable case studies. Educators tell us that one of the finest ways to teach children the multiplication tables, the spelling of difficult words, or the working of abstract problems is to wait until the child is asleep; then, sitting by the bedside, repeat over and over again the facts that need to be absorbed by the subconscious mind. Soon the child will discover, much to his delight, that he can master the problem. It is never wise to acquaint a child with what you are doing in this regard. It would be cruel to rob him of his sense of accomplishment. Also, the playing of tape recordings while a person sleeps has become a proved method of teaching.

In order to practice directive prayer to the subconscious mind of another person, one must follow a few simple rules: (1) You must speak as clearly as possible. Begin your prayer by stating the person's name three times in succession, in order that his subconscious mind will be aroused and open to your suggestions. (2) It is best to broadcast to the subject soon after he has gone to sleep so that the subconscious mind will have the entire night to dwell on the idea communicated. People in prayer groups may often broadcast throughout the night at specific times, but they should make sure that individually their messages are absolutely identical. (3) Keep the message simple but affirmative. A statement of God-centered intent must be sharp as a sword.

Occasionally I have the opportunity of preaching to

people in homes for the aged, and here I find men and women with great spiritual capacity, marking time until they die. This is a tragic waste of spiritual resources. One evening I addressed a sizeable crowd of aged people at a nearby Baptist home. I informed them of some of the most pressing world needs and urged them to stop thinking about themselves and get on with the unfinished work God is calling them to through directed prayer. I challenged them to establish prayer groups in their home. After the talk I was overwhelmed by the enthusiasm of those people. They were just waiting for such an idea. One lady rushed up, with a smile on her face, and exclaimed, "I've been waiting to hear a calling like this for years, now I know what I can do. I'm ninety-three years old and still able to serve the Lord."

The teen-agers, with their boundless energy and determination, are another untapped source of spiritual energy. If they can be taught early in life how to pray, just consider how powerfully God will use their lives through the years. We should never hesitate to bring young people onto the battleground of our spiritual offensive against the powers of darkness. Let them take their rightful places as responsible people of God. Too long we have denied our Christian youth the opportunity of participating in a spiritual crusade, because we were afraid they would fail.

Now, if you agree to the validity of the directed prayer approach, would it not seem a redemptive course of action for our troubled world to initiate a great directed prayer offensive? All people who believe in directed prayer should regularly transmit messages across the world to the Kremlin, Peiping, Cuba, and other places where evil is entenched. Furthermore, we should pray using all the visual aids at our disposal. We should use maps to spot locations for our praying, and other information including the names of people and institutions, and even pictures of persons that would help make more effective our visualizations as we pray. None of these artificial props for praying should ever become so indispensable that we find ourselves unable to pray without this extra paraphernalia, however. We must remain flexible and free to move at the prompting of the Holy Spirit.

Churches across America with already established prayer groups can develop a directed prayer offensive without involving any more additional organization. Individual Christians who believe in this approach ought to begin at once, and if they find a few other people who share a common belief in this method of prayer, perhaps a directed prayer group could be organized immediately.

I believe that our praying ought to be specific and sharp-edged. We should know for whom we are praying, why we're praying, and what we're praying for. If we don't know, and must invent a reason, then we should not continue. We need to trust the Holy Spirit to teach us how to approach each situation. We should pray the prayer for guidance in preparation for directed prayer. Too often we plunge headlong into prayer projects, spraying the air with pious-sounding petitions and missing the point of the whole matter. If several thousand prayer groups were to pray in a directed manner, under the guidance of the Holy Spirit, for a crucial world problem, the results would be glorious.

I can envisage a Congress of Prayer that would convene at least once a year in Washington, D. C., for the express purpose of concentrating spiritual energies on world problems. This assemblage would include representatives of prayer groups, spiritual life organizations, spiritual life retreats, from all denominations. The Congress of Prayer would not assemble to hear progress reports, eloquent speeches, and timewasting debates; rather it would be a gathering of prayers to pray believingly for specific target goals. We need not wait for a national Congress of Prayer to be inaugurated in Washington, D. C.; Christians in cities, towns, and hamlets all across America should establish local congresses of prayer at once.

The people addressing the national Congress of Prayer would be experienced in dealing with some phase of a particular world problem. Representatives of the State Department, using maps and giving important objective information, would be of invaluable assistance. They would offer the Prayer Congress pertinent facts concerning our prayer projects. Then the Prayer Congress would be led in prayer by spiritual life leaders who would serve as agents for the Holy Spirit in launching the delegates on the wings of prayer. Prayer congresses, under the leadership of the Holy Spirit, would be dedicated to the purpose of prayer in its various forms, and all other activities would be of secondary importance.

People returning home from the annual meeting of the Congress of Prayer doubtlessly would be inspired to establish prayer congresses in their own communities, if this has not already been accomplished. When world crisis situations arise, local congresses of prayer could be called into session across America, and people who believe in directed prayer and other forms of praying would gather together and pray for specific situations. The constituency of all congresses, national or local, should be nondenominational. The Holy Spirit is no respecter of denominational lines. Prayer is a gift of God and belongs to all his people. Congresses of prayer all over America, meeting to direct their prayers on given occasions toward specific target areas, would, by the power of the Holy Spirit, again and again change the course of human history. And if a national Prayer Congress should prove an effective instrument, why not an international Congress of Prayer?

Our responsibility to the world does not end here. A Congress of Prayer can release great power through the Holy Spirit, but this world has problems that require more than prayer alone. If all the world's hungry people were to be placed in a single line, they would circle the world twenty-five times. Each five seconds one of them dies of starvation, and that half of the world which goes to bed hungry every night is illiterate. The world population is growing faster than the supply of food coming in.

Frank Laubach, "Apostle to the Illiterates," has taught me that our incredible achievements in preventive medicine have nearly wiped out all the old epidemics that formerly killed millions of these starving illiterates. Smallpox, yellow fever, cholera, typhoid fever, bubonic plague, and diseases associated with childbirth, have been tremendously reduced, resulting in a population explosion.

Communists have a way of exploiting even the conditions of illiteracy and starvation to their advantage as they encourage these downtrodden people to do something about their tragic circumstances—start a revolution, overthrow the upper 10 per cent of the population who own the land, take over the country, redivide the wealth, and gain leadership. This is the utopian story of communism as it is preached by some half a million communist missionaries around the world, a large percentage of which are nationals returning to their homelands, cities, towns, and villages to evangelize for communism.

The Communists have cleverly recruited the most aggressive, articulate village leaders who are critical enough of their living condition to want to do something about it. These angry people are invited to spend some time in the Kremlin, where they are trained in communist propaganda methods, and then returned to their native countries full of fire and zeal for their new religion. No wonder the world is going communist at such a rapid pace. However persuasive the communist salesmen may be, the fact remains that they are extremely poor in making delivery. They may succeed in stirring up the masses of illiterate people, but only because these people cannot read an alternative point of view that would give them a basis for making a sound judgment. One day we may realize that the greatest threat to freedom throughout the world is not communism but illiteracy. It is not the literate countries that go communist, only the illiterate.

What can we do to stop the forward march of communism? We must go to the illiterates and teach them how to read and write; give them books on how to farm and run their machinery and how to take care of their homes and families. Then, guided through the power of literacy, they will discover for themselves the way to come up out of poverty and degradation. Communism promises all of this, but cannot and will not deliver it.

Part of our warfare against the dark powers is certainly on this educational front. However, with such a small army to send out, we are in constant retreat on the world battlefield. Frank Laubach, with thirty years of experience in this war on illiteracy, with his each-one-teach-one, "lightning literacy" method, has dispatched teams into some 101 countries and made primers in 300 languages. Laubach has proved his method, and the Laubach Literacy Foundation and other literacy organizations are doing an excellent piece of work; but unfortunately they are not doing enough, because they lack the vital resources of men and money.

Countries all over the world are clamoring for the Laubach teams to come in and teach. These countries are demanding, not begging for, the gift of literacy so they can become productive and creative people. They say, "Either give us literacy or we will go communist."

The churches of our country ought to rise to this challenge by sending out literacy experts, teachers, and technical missionaries wherever the need exists. Church leaders should put first things first by analyzing their budgets, eliminating the frills, operating with less staff, and employing more laymen for church work. They should stop the foolish spending on unnecessary equipment, expensive advertising, and the senseless stream of mimeographing and mailings.

Recently I was mailed a slick-back brochure from a church proudly announcing the purchase of a new pipe organ that cost approximately $67,000. The cost of this organ would have paid the yearly salaries of at least eight technical missionary families. Certainly a less expensive organ would have adequately served the purpose. Was this cost justified? Was it really a necessary expenditure in the light of tragic world need? People who would spend their money so wastefully ought to visit a mission field and see their ragged, illiterate, disease-ravaged, pinched-faced, starving brethren begging for a bite of bread.

In order to speed up the program of literacy education, Frank Laubach has been urging that people going overseas be given training in literacy teaching methods. For instance, military service personnel going overseas should be afforded this training, as should all foreign students who will be returning to their native lands. Missionary personnel from all denominations, professional government people, retired people, willing to give a year or more for the purpose of teaching illiterates, and tourists should be given literacy teacher training.

The financial sponsorship for dispatching literacy experts and underwriting literacy projects could come from churches, schools, and universities; industry; service organizations; and government as well. If you are interested in getting further information on literacy projects simply write the Laubach Literacy Foundation, 235 East 22nd Street, New York, New York, or contact your denominational headquarters and make inquiry.

Literacy is not the only answer to the enormous need of the underprivileged half of the world. Several organizations, such as C.R.O.P. (Christian Rural Overseas Program), Heifer Project, Church World Service, CARE, (Cooperative for American Relief Everywhere),

World Neighbors, Association for International Development, Medico, Inc., Carnegie Corporation, Ford Foundation, and Rockefeller Foundation—to name only a few—are making vital contributions to needy people around the world. Their help includes health, education, agriculture, technical, economic, medical aid and assistance. Other groups, including church and service organizations along with individual support, are continuing a tremendous program of people-to-people compassion.

The church I serve is involved in the Army of Compassion movement, which is a program designed to recruit technical missionaries for overseas service and raise funds to underwrite their expenses. The financing of a technical missionary family is borne by "companies"—150 people giving a dollar per week comprise a company. The companies are organized in churches, schools, fraternal organizations, clubs, and industries across the nation. The Army of Compassion is not a denominational program. Money collected is sent directly to any mission board or other dispatching agency that will send out technical people wherever the need exists. At present our church is giving spiritual and financial support to a technical missionary family in Bolivia, who are agriculture experts involved in community development. This venture in compassion has profoundly influenced the life of our parish.

All of these programs I have previously mentioned are rendering great service. Health advancement is a monumental achievement. The programs of community development, agricultural and industrial, have been of significant benefit. However, the fact remains that an underdeveloped

73

country is a country of underdeveloped people. No amount of outside assistance can do for the underdeveloped what they must do for themselves. This is not a criticism of any aid or assistance program. The point is that if these people are to ever come up out of their misery, they must first be literate. One of the great frustrations of agricultural and technical experts working in countries of great need is that illiterates do not make good farmers or able technicians. It is the illiterate half of the world that is poverty stricken and hungry. For this reason I have spent so much time emphasizing the need for literacy outreach throughout the world.

We can begin to meet the needs of the illiterates and other desperate people of the world with marvelous results, but only if we keep our hearts warm with the presence of Christ. If we are attempting to do these good missionary works for no better reason than to save our own skins, then our very works will bring a judgment upon us. Certainly faith without works is dead, but works without faith is equally dead.

Charles Malik, the distinguished statesman from Lebanon, has said, "Why don't you Americans who have such a magnificent spiritual heritage proclaim your faith to the world? Why are you forever trying to beat the Russians with Russian weapons, giving the impression to all the world that you put more trust in material forces than you do in your own dynamic Christian beliefs in freedom and the dignity of man which is what the whole world really wants?"

How easy it is to be distracted from the essence of our calling in Christ, as we are faced with the enormous

74

problem of how we should organize our efforts in order to do the Lord's work. My suggestions for developing congresses of prayer and giving greater support for literacy work and technical missionary projects across the world could bring about the creation of additional mechanized activity, distracting us from our high calling and becoming an end in itself. In my nightmares I see organizational wheels within wheels moving ever faster and eventually operating independently of whatever might be the will of God. Organizational activities can become so complicated and demanding that they develop an immunity to criticism and resistance to change. One reason why the Alcoholics Anonymous movement is so eminently successful in arresting the drinking problem of countless men and women across our country is because A. A. has deliberately resolved to forbid organizational distractions from impeding its spiritual mission.

We must recognize that inattention to spiritual goals arises from much more than a simple involvement in the quagmire of organizational activities. For instance, there is nothing that so stifles spiritual development for a person or group than the habitual handling of holy things with mechanical detachment and routine indifference.

In the Christian faith the distractions, like temptations, flow in from all sides. As the writer of the book of Hebrews put it: "At a time when you should be teaching others, you need teachers yourselves to repeat to you the ABC of God's revelation to men. You have become people who need a milk diet and cannot face solid food! For anyone who continues to live on 'milk' is obviously im-

75

mature—he simply has not grown up" (Heb. 5:12-13, Phillips).

If we are painfully honest we will see how we have become distracted from the essentials of a continuing close consciousness of our Lord and his leading. Of course, there are the shining moments of high inspiration when we are swept heavenward into a great spiritual experience, but what about the rest of the time? When our spiritual attention is diverted by other things, we forget to tend the fires of the Spirit.

The greatest danger in our Christian life is that we become so absorbed in service to the church or some agency of the church that we forget the living presence of Christ. There is a vivid analogy to this idea in the spiritual significance of Pierre Boulle's novel, *Bridge Over the River Kwai*. This story concerns a captive battalion of British soldiers who, under the leadership of their colonel, constructed a bridge to be used by their captors— the Japanese. The colonel became so absorbed in building the bridge that he actually forgot that the bridge belonged to the enemy; that his country was at war with the Japanese; and that eventually the bridge must be destroyed.

The analogy fits the Christian church almost perfectly. A friend came to my office and told me an almost unbelievable story. He spoke of a man, known to both of us, who for several years was a great spiritual leader in our city. Today this man is a lost soul, having become so distracted from his ministry for Christ by whisky, loose women, and wealth that he has allowed himself to be led down the rocky path to hell. When confronted by my friend's searching question, "What happened to you?" he replied, "My church has become a social club. I was hungry for spiritual food and did not have a place to feed my spirit. I wasn't strong enough to find help by myself." The starving spirit of this man should haunt every ordained salaried lecturer and every church lecture association; every churchly head manager and every ecclesiastical club; every pious business director and every socializing parish, until they are all brought under the judgment of God.

If we are to undertake directive prayer projects for crisis situations, establish congresses of prayer, and move with greater numbers and financial resource in the war of amazing kindness against illiteracy, starvation, and poverty, we must make a journey to Pentecost. Church organizations, denominational machinery, diluted Christian culture, and pulpit oratory are not the answer. The modern-day church, on its knees praying for an outpouring of the Holy Spirit, is our only hope in doing the will of God through the purposed instruments set forth in this chapter. Only through the power of the Holy Spirit can prophecy ring true—our words catch fire—our plans glow—our prayers sparkle—and our hearts burn within us.

4

Life and Death

Made like Him, like Him we rise . . .
Ours the cross, the grave, the skies.

—Charles Wesley

"So it is that Christianity," said Soren Kierkegaard, "has taught the Christian to think dauntlessly of everything earthly and worldly, including death." Paul has said it even more profoundly: "All things are yours," including, "life and death . . . and you are Christ's; and Christ is God's."

Paul's enthusiasm for both life and death was based entirely on his relationship to Christ. No doubt he would have preferred to die and come into the fullness of God's glory, but for him death would have been a pleasant means of escape. It would have been impossible for Paul to evade the great needs of this world by simply ignoring the stupendous fact that God so loved the world that he gave his only begotten Son, even to the death of a cross to save it. Despite his imprisonment, beatings, stoning, shipwrecks, peril, and pain, Paul chose to live for Christ. As he said it, "For me to live is Christ"—and Christ is all.

When we come to possess the spirit that was in Paul,

we shall seek the kingdom of God without an ulterior motive. This was the spirit that lived in the sainted woman whom Ulrich Zwingli told about, who walked the streets of Strasbourg with a flaming torch in one hand and a pail of water in the other. When asked what she was doing she answered that with the torch she was going to burn the lovely furniture of heaven, and with the pail of water she was going to put out the flames of hell, so that in the future people would love the Lord for himself alone, and not for the rewards of heaven nor the fear of hell.

One reason some people have such a terrible fear of death is because the ego is proudly enthroned at the center of their lives. The ego, or "Big I," trembles at the thought of death, because this represents the ultimate threat to selfhood as we understand it. The "Big I" writes itself prominently in correspondence, mentions itself incessantly in conversation, draws attention to itself by faultfinding and criticism, seeks the applause of the crowd, and attempts to impress others in a variety of ways. There was a certain "Big I" man having marital difficulty, who simply could not comprehend why his wife would leave him after he had purchased her a $300 set of matched golf clubs, paid for her professional golf lessons, and bought her a $4,000 automobile just to show his love. Surely, he reasoned, she should have been impressed.

The "Big I" monopolizes every conversation, holds forth in long-winded speeches when serving on boards or committees, enjoys quoting from learned people and using an erudite vocabulary that will send folks rushing to the nearest dictionary to find out what has been said.

79

Obscenities, profanity, and all the other attention-getting mechanisms mark well the "Big I" person with a certain label that all can read.

Dean Inge once said, "The person who seems to be perpetually complimenting himself for being what he is, without any visible ground for his extreme satisfaction, puts those who associate with him into an uncharitable state of mind."

God's great people are free of "Big I" trouble. They are not enslaved to the world's most demanding dictator. Rather, they have found, through surrendering "Big I" to God, that he has given them access to freedom they never would have experienced while enslaved to self— freedom from the tortuous demand of needing to impress people, freedom from the necessity of needing to attract attention, and freedom from worshiping the applause of men. These are blessed liberties. The question before God's free people is not what do others think of us, but rather what does God think of us? Free men in the Lord pray, "O God, I want to do your will, think your thoughts, see what you want me to see, hear what you want me to hear, and speak what you want me to speak. In other words I want you to live through me." Some people might consider this a form of slavery, and this is a valid observation. However, slavery to God produces real freedom, because the demanding "Big I" has been crucified. The only way that leads to abundant life is by way of the Cross that will break the back of our sins, lacerate our pride, and hammer our egos to a pulp. Our identity as the person God created is released in fullness when the "Big I" of egocentricity, or what we are not, is crucified.

Nicodemus came to Jesus as a seeker of truth; the sort of intellectual truth one collects to gain a fine reputation, not the power of truth that shakes the foundation of a person's life. At first Nicodemus attempted to flatter Jesus by referring to him as a "teacher come from God," and saying, "For no one can do these signs that you do, unless God is with him." Jesus answered him, "Truly, truly, I say to you, unless one is born anew, he cannot see the kingdom of God" (John 3:2-3).

Jesus had not softened the blow. The "Big I" must die so that the new life can be born. "How can a man be born when he is old?" cried Nicodemus. Jesus answered, "Unless one is born of water and the Spirit, he cannot enter the kingdom of God. That which is born of the flesh is flesh, and that which is born of the Spirit is spirit. Do not marvel that I said to you, 'You must be born anew' " (John 3:4, 5-7).

A man's entire being must be born again, changed, transformed. The old cannot contain the new; the old must decrease that the new may increase. "The wind blows where it will, and you hear the sound of it, but you do not know whence it comes or whither it goes; so it is with every one who is born of the Spirit." (John 3:8.) Nicodemus disappeared into the darkness, mumbling to himself. I wonder if he did not understand more of what Jesus told him than we have been led to believe. Mark Twain once commented that the sections of the Bible which gave him the most difficulty were the ones he understood only too well.

The statements of Jesus are clear enough. The old order must die to make room for the new. This requires new birth. The doors of old life must be opened inward that new life may enter. There are doors to rooms of existing death that must be flung open in business life, family life, sex life, school life, church life, and in community life so that we may have new life. There are little centers of hate, puffed egos, damning prejudices, irritating discords, petty jealousies, stubborn prides, pampered emotions, nurtured indulgences that need to be crucified so we can live for Christ.

In Christ's parable of the sower, seeds, and soils we get a vivid picture of the ways people resist crucifixion of self that they might have what they chose to call life. In one scene of the parable some seed fell among the thorny bushes that choked off the tender sprouts as they emerged. There are people desperately hungry to come up into new life in Christ, but they have allowed the thorny vines of self-seeking and serving to so entwine their lives that their very spirits are in danger of being choked to death. Why don't they take the vine in hand and free themselves? In order to do this they would need to let go of the overrated pleasures of this world and desire the holy life and breath more than death and decay.

Jesus put it this way, "He who does not take his cross and follow me is not worthy of me. He who finds his life will lose it, and he who loses his life for my sake will find it" (Matt. 10:38-39). But let me hasten to point out that it is not enough to come before the presence of the Lord emptied, crucified, and bleeding; now we must seek the infilling of the Holy Spirit that we can be born anew and enter the new life.

There is something within us that must die before something else can be born. Paul was fond of calling his unconverted sinning self the "old self." He had other appropriate expressions for his "old sinful nature" that constantly opposed his highest resolve, mocked his holy purpose, scoffed at his divine seeking, and belittled the power of God at work in him. In the book of Romans, Paul says, "Wretched man that I am! Who will deliver me from this body of death?" (Rom. 7:24.) No doubt "body of death" referred to a ghastly method of capital punishment used by the Roman authorities, which consisted in the binding of a corpse to a condemned criminal, face to face, eye to eye, mouth to mouth, cheek to cheek, and limb to limb. The living man was forced to carry the rotting body of death until its foul corruption eventually killed him.

The old self continually attacks the soul of man through "the sin which clings so closely" (Heb. 12:1). Unconverted "little sins," as we call them, such as prejudice, anger, pride, vanity, deceit, falsehood, gossip, and so forth, should give abundant proof of the tremendous need in our lives for crucifixion of the old self. The satanic strategy for mastery is discernible whenever we attempt to disassociate our "little sins" from our "old self" that is so terribly in need of repentance and transformation.

If the demonic power would take a voice he might say: "You say you want to be a Christian and have a new life —very well, choose a reasonable method. Join a church and try hard to learn about Christ, then strive to follow his example. Study his words and ways and work at it until you're thoroughly frustrated. Discover for yourself that the gospel is not good news at all except for those who by nature are inclined to thinking about ideals, devotion, responsibility, and sacrifice." Indeed, the unconverted "old self," or the "Big I," loves ideals and sacrifice, intellectualizing and externalizing, good works, festivals and lawn fetes, theatrics and orations, benevolences, organization, and church machinery. The "old self" glows in the presence of gushing rhetoric from the Sunday morning pulpit or teaching lectern and all the sermonettes for Christianettes on the road to heavenette.

The satanic scheme is obvious when reduced to its simplest terms. The old self magnifies all that is natural and ignores all that is supernatural. Therefore, the old self will so minimize the significance of going deeper in the Christian faith that at best a man will remain a marginal Christian, putting Christ somewhere other than at the center of his life. There are multitudes of quasi-Chrisian people whose souls' song is sung in a minor key. What a sorry commentary these people write on the Christian faith, without the living power of God, without the exuberance of faith, without the radiance of the Holy Spirit, and without praise for the Lord.

The question here is as old as time itself. When will you repent, crucify your "Big I" in the name and nature of Jesus Christ, and receive the Holy Spirit? Christ came for this purpose and died for this cause. Are you willing to die so that he may live in you? Jesus said, "I am the resurrection and the life: he that believeth in me, though he were dead, yet shall he live: and whosoever liveth and believeth in me shall never die." (John 11:25-26, KJV). When the "old self" is crucified, a resurrection happens; a new being is born by the power of the Holy Spirit; and what was old is made new by the Spirit's infilling in the quickening of one's whole being and the development of spiritual sensitivities. When the Holy Spirit comes upon a person, he will experience a total rejuvenation that will flow through his entire being. This experience must be a foretaste of what will happen to us in the final resurrection beyond this life.

The healing ministry brings into sharp focus the experience of resurrection of death to life. What final good is it for a person to have his eyesight restored, a growth removed, his anxiety eased, or to be told that an antibiotic may do its work, or that the surgical operation is a success, if the spirit of the person is still in the clutches of death and destruction? I am in favor of keeping spiritually dead patients alive for one purpose, and that is that they be resurrected into life, and I believe our healing prayers should begin by ministering to the sick person's spirit.

I shall never forget the first healing service held in our church. It was on a Sunday afternoon, and our subject was one of our leading women, who requested that we pray concerning a rigid tumor, the size of a hen's egg, that had been detected growing within her. Over a period of two months she had been examined seven times by three specialists, who unanimously agreed that an operation was imperative. After the service she entered the hospital and was examined again and the verdict was the same. On the day of the operation I entered her room at approximately 5:30 A.M. The sight that met my eyes was incredible. The woman was softly singing to herself, praising God for the nurses, the doctors, the hospital, and praying for all the patients in the hospital. At first I thought my eyes were

85

playing tricks on me, but her face seemed to glow as though illumined by an unearthly radiance, and it remained that way. Within a few moments we were praying together, and soon her prayers took the wings of morning and ascended to the heights. "Oh God, I am not praying for the removal of a little tumor. You could take that away in a matter of moments, but what I am praying for is a complete cleansing and a new birth. Heal all of me, every part. Please give me a total healing of Spirit, heart, mind—and body. Make me whole for thee." She had prayed for the resurrection of her spirit.

Within an hour after returning to my office I was called back to the hospital. The woman's room was a strange scene of bewildered people coming and going. I could only get a few words of sense from the people standing about. It seems that after she had been taken to the operating room and the doctors were assembled, one of them decided to make one final examination before operating. And behold, they discovered that overnight the tumor had reduced in size so dramatically that an operation was unnecessary. The doctors were completely mystified, the nurses were baffled, and the family was overwhelmed. All were amazed, except the woman who lay on her bed, filled with the Holy Spirit, made whole and resurrected to new life; and she was still praising the Lord.

I have noticed that when people turn to the church and request a healing ministry, the extent of their expectation is a pastoral call with a few well-chosen words of comfort and a nice sympathetic prayer. But no one really expects the church to heal in the name of Christ, and certainly no one would be so presumptuous as to suggest that a sick person needs a resurrection experience.

One of the most revealing passages concerning healing in the New Testament appears in the fifth chapter of James:

Is any one among you suffering? Let him pray. Is any cheerful? Let him sing praise. Is any among you sick? Let him call for the elders of the church, and let them pray over him, anointing him with oil in the name of the Lord; and a prayer of faith will save the sick man, and the Lord will raise him up; and if he has committed sins, he will be forgiven. Therefore confess your sins to one another, and pray for one another, that you may be healed (James 5:13-16).

I can scarcely imagine someone calling for the elders of a modern-day church and requesting them to come and pray for the sick and resurrect the dead. Most official bodies of the church have relegated all that kind of work to the pastor or some dear soul who is by nature inclined to go visiting the sick. The consequence of this is a terrible neglect in the sacramental life of the church, actually further burying in irrelevancy the hope of Christ for the world, which is a redemptive people of God carrying on his ministry. In our church we are attempting to revive that lost ministry.

There was a certain woman critically ill with hepatitis, who called me and requested that I visit her in the hospital. I had not been with her for more than a few moments when she candidly described the seriousness of her illness and admitted with complete frankness that she would soon be dead. However, she seemed to be reaching out with unfaltering faith that somehow I would be able to help her. At that time I had only an elementary acquaintanceship with the field of spiritual healing, but I had ventured far enough to know that a brisk, two-minute prayer and a hand-holding utterance of godly concern would be a betrayal to her faith. Amazingly her faith was like a great magnet reaching out to me and summoning forth the words that she needed to hear. I talked to her at great length about being receptive and perfectly responsive to Christ's love and his desire to make her whole.

I did not pray for this woman's complete healing at once; rather, we determined to take one step at a time. Little by little she surrendered herself to God's will, displacing an unhealthy emotional pattern with the creative energies of love. I gave her some books to read, one of them, *Be Thou Made Whole,* by Glenn Clark. In this book he outlines a program of several baths for healing of the body, mind, and spirit. Each subsequent day that I visited her I could see the positive signs of returning health. I saw death overcome as the life-giving forces of love and peace evidenced themselves in a miraculous physical regeneration. Within a few weeks she returned to her home, came back to church, and in a short time was teaching a church-school class and attending a Yokefellow group. Here again we have witnessed a resurrection experience.

In each case that I have described there was an underlying emotional disturbance causing the illness. Yet the patient was physically sick. Yielding of self in a specific way was the key to healing. It would not have been enough just to pray in a general way for the patient's return to health. Something was also required from the person to be healed, and that was an eagerness to be cleansed of whatever was causing the problem, and a willingness to surrender it in confession. There can be no true healing in giving or receiving unless there is a corresponding seeking of God's forgiveness for our sins and a willingness to accept his healing love. Indeed, the life of wholeness is the forgiven life. As the Holy Communion ritual puts it, we repent of our sins and intend to lead a new life. Something must die before something new can live.

The resurrection spirit entering a person transforms utterly. The most obvious change that occurs in a person who has come from death to life is the way that he presents himself. He no longer needs to pretend, to pose, and parade. He is freed from the necessity of trying to make a big impression and gain the attention of others. These former things have passed away. I wonder if Heywood Broun didn't have these empty, superficial ways of men in mind when he declined an invitation to a school reunion by saying, "I don't like to eat with dead men." Perhaps we've all had the experience of being with people who did nothing more than rattle their dead bones in order to be noticed.

The infilling of the Holy Spirit takes away our selfish desire for place, power, and reputation and displaces it with a holy longing to be of useful service to others. In the spiritual dimension personal greatness cannot be defined in terms of prestige and glory, but rather in individual self-giving. On that fateful journey to Jerusalem, when Jesus would be delivered up to crucifixion, his disciples were quarreling about the places of honor in the kingdom of God. Gently our Lord rebuked them by saying: "Whoever would be first among you must be your slave; even as the Son of man came not to be served but to serve, and to give his life as a ransom for many" (Matt. 20:27-28).

When the disciples were finally filled with the Holy Spirit, they no longer had an itch for first place in the kingdom; instead they had developed a tremendous passion to win the world for Christ. Beverly Carradine used to say that this new life had for him "quenched an un-Christlike ambition. It makes one willing to be overlooked and unknown. The fever for place and prominence is taken out." And turned in this new spiritual direction our aspirations to sit at the "right hand or the left hand" of Christ in glory are now refocused to the hope and prayer that we might sit where Mary sat, at the feet of Jesus.

Paul's words seem appropriate here:

Have this mind among yourselves, which you have in Christ Jesus, who, though he was in the form of God, did not count equality with God a thing to be grasped, but emptied himself, taking the form of a servant, being born in the likeness of man. And being found in human form he humbled himself and became obedient unto death, even death on a cross. . . . That at the name of Jesus every knee should bow, in heaven and on earth and under the earth, and every tongue confess that Jesus Christ is Lord, to the glory of God the Father (Phil. 2:5-11).

90

But how do we look at death? Doesn't it seem the ultimate threat ever set over against us? Are we not more likely to concur with Mephistopheles, who said, "Death is never quite a welcome friend," than to join Paul's triumphant chorus that joyously proclaims, "All things are yours," including life and death?

Most of us still bear spiritual kinship with the king of Northumbria who, thirteen hundred years ago in a court hall ablaze with firelight from a hundred torches, proceeded to ask the first Christian missionaries who visited England: "Can this new religion tell us anything of what happens after death? The soul of man is like a sparrow flying through this lighted hall. It enters at one door from the darkness outside, flits through the light and warmth and passes out at the further end into the dark again. Can this new religion solve for us the mystery? What happens to men after death, in the dim unknown?"

It was reported several years ago that two English explorers had discovered a tomb in the Egyptian desert at least four thousand years old. On entering the place of burial they found a sarcophagus on which were inscribed these words: "O my life, my love, my little one! Would God I had died for thee." For a moment the two explorers entered the grief experience of heartbroken parents who long ago lay to rest their little one. With uncovered heads the Englishmen sealed the entrance to the tomb, and in respectful silence left in repose the timeless grave hidden in the desert.

I have stood beside the grief-stricken, staring with them into the face of death, and on occasion have heard them speak in the vein of Robert Ingersoll as he lamented the passing of his brother: "Life is a narrow vale between the mountain peaks of two eternities. . . . The skies give back no sound. . . . We cry aloud and the only answer is the echo of our wailing cry."

I have played my part in the game of make-believe when the angel of death hovers near; refusing to talk of death, even to acknowledge its imminent presence. At one time or another most people become pretenders against the grim fact of death. Our pretenses suggest that death is too morbid a subject for healthy-minded people to discuss, and we must evade in every conceivable way the harsh implications of its meaning. So when a loved one becomes desperately ill, if we do not believe in divine healing, we contrive to deceive that person as to the gravity of his illness. However, all the masquerading in the world will not hold back the bad news when family and friends, doctors and nurses whisper their poisonous pessimisms within the conscious or subconscious hearing of the patient.

When a person does die he is entrusted to the care of a friendly mortician who will exercise considerable theatrical skills in staging a funeral performance, complete with make-up, costuming, music, scenery, and dialogue for all who will attend. Layout night in some sections of our country is rapidly becoming a social institution, as gregarious people crowd into the display rooms to gather near costly coffins and behold the embalmer's decorative art. Now and then you will hear them exclaim perceptively, "Doesn't he look natural?" "Doesn't she look wonderful, almost better than she did when alive?" "She's probably better off now." "He looks like he is just sleeping."

The next day the preacher arrives and delivers his best funeral sermon, which often sounds faintly apologetic. Many ministers reason that it is their responsibility to defend the ways of the Lord, and death puts the burden of proof squarely on them. Remembering his seminary training the pastor will guard against mentioning the words death, die, or dead; neither will he mention the deceased by name, nor call attention to the present moment of sorrow.

If someone were to calculate the cost of the carloads of flowers that are delivered for the average funeral, the amount would prove astonishing. I have never grown accustomed to such profligate waste as we see spent on cut flowers for funeral services. I passionately begrudge the money so notoriously misused for a purpose that is by any measure singularly unchristian.

The scene of the modern-day service for burial of the dead has moved from the church to the more convenient funeral home. I have been told that the most practical and appropriate place for the service is the elegantly draped viewing room, where family and friends will not be distracted. I cannot agree that the symbols of a living faith could be classified as distractions. Also there is the practical consideration of so much extra effort connected with getting in and out of the church.

The brightly polished black hearse waits at the curbstone for the pallbearers to deposit the casket on a cushioned platform through the sidesaddle door. At last the casket sits resplendent in the hearse, bedecked by a large host of flowers. A fifty-dollar spray of roses with "Dear old Dad" spelled out in golden letters on a crimson scarf adds a certain sentimental touch. I still remember one such inscription—"Good Luck Mother."

Under a canopied area a grave has been freshly dug in the dark earth, and the pile of extra dirt is well-hidden beneath a covering of artificial grass. There the words of the Committal are solemnly said, while the memorial garden chimes usually play something sentimental such as "In the Sweet By and By." Gravediggers, hiding behind thick trees so as not to be seen by the mourners, will soon reappear, lower the casket into the vault, remove the green grass, and cover the vault with the good brown earth.

A man was ill, finally died, and has been buried, but at no time has anyone said what needs to be said. The reality of death has been evaded by substituting euphemisms for fact. Death, the most unpopular word in the world, is given another name or expression more pleasing to the ear. We say that a person has gone to his final rest, passed away, slipped beyond, taken his final sleep, gone West, headed for the last roundup, kicked the bucket, cashed in his chips, gone to his reward; or more elegantly, as Shakespeare said, "shuffled off this mortal coil."

But the truth of the matter is simply this—if there is no death there can be no life. All of life is filled with the punctuation marks of death—commas, hyphens, semicolons, question marks, exclamation points, even periods —all indicating that there is more to come. If a man is afraid of death, then he is afraid of life. Each moment of our life is punctuated by a creative urge to die to something so that we may live to something else. There is a purposefulness about creative dying. In the economy of God's plan for us, we die from an old level to a more advanced development. An infant dies to a toddler, a toddler dies to a young child, a young child dies to a teen-ager, a teen-ager dies to a young adult, a young adult dies to an older adult, and the older adult dies—provided the process has not been interrupted—to move into life eternal.

Death is the instrument of our becoming. The price of becoming is death. If death is seen through the eyes of faith, it will be received as with the welcome joy of St. Francis: "Be Thou praised, My Lord, for our Sister Bodily Death." If death can be seen as a process that keeps life moving to something greater than before, then its sting diminishes. No sane person would choose to have his development arrested at the level of a baby, a child, a teen-ager, a young adult, or an older adult. Life cries out for completeness, perfection, for God. We may attempt to retard the erosion of age by trying to preserve the appearance of youth, through the use of hair dyes, wrinkle removers, chin straps, magic creams and oils, pencil and paint, steam baths, gymnasiums, sunbaths, and plastic surgery. But the fact remains that wrinkles, gray hair, and the settling condition of age should faithfully convict a person that he is going ahead to something from which he will not return. The door of life between today and tomorrow is ajar, but the door of death between today and yesterday is forever closed. We cannot go back to yesterday on account of regret for past sin or remorse for lost opportunity, nor can we go into tomorrow by taking anxious thought. There is nothing on which we need to concentrate more attention than the wonderful present, encompassed in the strong hands of God in which we live, move, die, and have our being. If life is centered in God, then through death we grow up into his likeness. And so we come to life's most intriguing question, about which most of us would like to be better informed. What sort of life lies behind the last door we call death?

Our only full authority in this matter is Jesus Christ who, strangely enough, was rather silent on the subject of how to picture the next life. Only now and then did he lift the veil between this life and the next, and then only for a brief moment. On the cross he consoled a dying thief crucified next to him. When that man prayed, "Jesus, remember me when you come in your kingly power." Jesus said to him not "perhaps," not "maybe," but, "Truly, I say to you, today you will be with me in Paradise" (Luke 23:42-43). In an upper room Jesus, speaking to his disciples, said, "In my Father's house are many rooms; if it were not so, would I have told you that I go to prepare a place for you?" (John 14:2.) This statement would seem to indicate that heaven consists of many communities and after death men enter the community in which they will have spiritual affinity. Therefore, it appears that our spiritual development in this life will in large measure determine where we begin to live in the next life. The room or community in which we shall dwell when entering heaven is not determined in one catastrophic moment of swift decision. Unlike a hotel registrar, God does not assign us our dwelling place in the next life; we assign ourselves in this life. The way we think and act; our basic desires and attitudes; and, above all, our spiritual development will determine where we shall begin in the life to come. How could it be otherwise? God condemns no one to hell, nor does he bless anyone to heaven; we ourselves are moment by moment preparing our future assignment. A person who has never practiced the presence of God would feel as unrelated to the celestial kingdom as a blind man attending an art exhibit. He would feel rebuked, inferior, and uncomfortable in the presence of those who have grown in spiritual understanding.

On one occasion, as it is recorded in the Scriptures, Jesus raised the curtain of heaven by his response to a certain situation. By reading between the lines of the experience, we are able to see, if only for a breath-taking second, something so appealing that it arouses more than a little curiosity concerning the place called paradise. Lazarus was dead. He was the brother of Mary and Martha of Bethany, all of whom were Jesus' friends. When word came of Lazarus' death, Jesus made his way to Bethany, and after arriving was told that Lazarus had been entombed for four days. Tearfully Mary and Martha lamented to Jesus that if he had been there Lazarus would not have died. Now as Jesus approached the tomb a host of Jews were still keeping vigil, for this was their custom. Standing at the edge of the crowd Jesus began to weep, and great tears began rolling down his face. There was a murmur in the crowd. One man said, "Look how much he loved him," and another commented, "Look, he is weeping for the loss of his friend Lazarus." But I declare to you, their observations were entirely wrong. Jesus wept that day in Bethany, not because of the death of his friend, but because of what he felt under obligation to do for the sake of his unknowing friends. He was tortured with sadness that he would need to bend down before a tomb filled with the stench of decay and call a man back from paradise—from a place where there is no more pain, nor loneliness, nor anxiety and distress, nor frustration and worry, nor sickness and despair. A place where there is no more death. Jesus wept because he needed to call a man back from heaven in all its glory—perfection and fulfillment.

Where is heaven? The question is a baffling one. We are too sophisticated to believe that heaven is up in the sky or down in the ground. We affirm without great enthusiasm that heaven is within us and that heaven is the place where God dwells. We more or less accept the truth of these statements, but we are not quite sure of what they mean.

One of the few things I remember from my high-school science courses is the fascinating fact of molecular activity. All things we see appearing to have solid form and substance are in reality combinations of little molecules moving so fast that it is impossible to see them except in a conglomerate state. Any mass object is in reality a collectivity of molecular movement. If, for some improbable reason, molecular activity should cease, then every material substance would vanish.

One day, while casually observing the action of a circulating air fan, I noted the illusion of a solid mass given off by the swiftly moving fan blades. But when I disconnected the fan from the electrical current, the blades ceased to move and the appearance of activity was no more. In an identical manner the physical world is largely illusionary. I believe that the spiritual world is the reality, and at the moment of our physical death we shall begin to see the actuality of the life that is all around us but has been hidden from us because of our physical limitations. Heaven is not another place, but only another state of consciousness. We are, as the writer of the book of Hebrews puts it, "surrounded by a great host of witnesses" (Heb. 12:1). Heaven is that eternal life which encompasses our mortal existence and is no farther from us than our next breath.

Because of this I have little difficulty believing the amazing story one of our leading churchwomen related to me the other day. She told about a friend of hers who was walking home one night along a dangerous, dimly lighted street where several thefts had recently taken place. Suddenly her friend noticed the threatening appearance of a man standing in a doorway a short distance ahead. Instantly he began to pray for God's presence to guide him along the street ahead. The next day while reading the morning newspaper he discovered a news item to the effect that someone coming along that same street at nearly the same hour had been robbed and beaten, but fortunately the thief had been apprehended. Unable to contain his curiosity, this man went to the city jail and received permission to visit the robber. He asked, "Were you standing in a doorway last night and did you see me pass by?" "Yes," replied the prisoner. "Why didn't you attempt to rob me—I was all alone." After a pause, the man behind bars responded, "No, you had a friend with you—and I never try to take two men at once." Talk about guardian angels!

Such spiritual manifestations are no longer considered to be only within the province of the witch doctor, charlatan, and crackpot; rather, they are rapidly becoming the subjects of scientific investigation. We Christians consider our declarations of personal survival after death to be very bold and challenging, but contemporary scientists are making bolder, more courageous statements than we ever dreamed of uttering.

For instance, scientists in the Oxford, England, laboratories under George de la Warr are saying that nothing is lost that has come to pass on this planet. The history of human life on earth is faithfully recorded in what is known as the Akashic Screen. All experience is retained in the ether, which is the vast subconscious storehouse of the world's experience. These men of science tell us that a machine has now been invented that will photograph events that happened years ago, and one day we shall be able to see the past on a television screen. Can you imagine watching Moses on Mt. Sinai, Elijah on Mt. Carmel, Nehemiah rebuilding the temple, Jesus emerging from the tomb in his resurrection body, the Pentecost experience, Peter preaching in Jerusalem, and Paul preaching on the Acropolis in Athens?

Norman Vincent Peale was telling about an article he had read in a parapsychology journal concerning a strange occurrence in England some time ago, before Telestar. One evening the viewing audience of Britain saw the call letters KLEE, Houston, Texas, on their television screens. Filled with delight, many of the British televiewers wrote letters to the Houston station expressing their appreciation for the fine transmission, only to discover after much inquiry that the television station KLEE had been off the air for three years. Where had the television signal come from? I think we may be on the way to explaining this phenomenon, and greater things than these shall we see in this new age.

A question that has aroused the curiosity of most people is whether or not communication is possible between this world and the next. I shall long remember the day Sherwood Eddy, the distinguished Christian leader, addressing the student body in our seminary chapel, announced matter-of-factly that he was in contact with a man who had been dead for several years. I am certain that anyone with a lesser reputation than Dr. Eddy would have been "laughed out of school." The chapel crowd listened in stunned silence to a report from beyond the grave. The discarnate had informed Sherwood Eddy that heaven is a place of creative work, progressive spiritual development, dynamic joyous adventure, wonderful sharing, and above all the love of God interpenetrating all.

There is a correspondence between this world and the next. What we have seen in the imperfection of this world will be seen in the perfect counterpart in heaven. Therefore heaven is a thrillingly beautiful place, more perfect and glorious than we could possibly imagine, for it is the dwelling place of the Author of perfection.

In answer to the question of whether communication is possible with those who have gone ahead into the larger life, I have heard Christian leaders reply, "We should not look for miraculous demonstrations in order to believe

in immortality. Faith in God does not require proof."
Other leaders have said, "Communicating with the dead
cannot be accepted as a valid theory because it does not
rest on any existing laws." I agree, we do not need repeated dazzling proofs to believe in immortality. In the
life, death, and resurrection of Jesus Christ we have
eternal life; life that begins here and now.

Furthermore, I do not believe that we can reasonably
accept the validity of certain phenomena that is not under-
girded by proved law, else the whole structure of life loses
its sense and balance. But what if there are certain laws,
other than natural laws, that are equally faithful and
well-established in the spiritual order? And consider the
possibility of the Holy Spirit's willingness to give us the
extrasensory gifts of healing, prophecy, speaking in
tongues, distinguishing between spirits, working miracles,
etc. Perhaps we are restricting God when he is willing to
go beyond the limitations we have placed on him.

The Bible is filled with the accounts of God talking to
men, angelic appearances, manifestations of spirits, spirit
infilling, visions, raising of the dead, and other such experience. Many modern Bible scholars attempt to reduce
the otherworldly material in the Scriptures to the plausible
hypotheses that the Hebrew writers were prone to ex-
aggerate the miraculous and embroider on the truth, or
the Hebrew manner of speaking is highly symbolic and
full of Oriental imagery which must not be taken literally. Let me hasten to protest this sort of scholarly specu-
lative nonsense. Once when our world was young and
silence enveloped this planet like a soft cloud, man's spiritual sensitivities were more highly developed than is the

102

case today. The old Hebrew may have been ignorant of biblical higher criticism, scientific materialism, and philosophical rationalism, but he knew what it was like to be visited by an angel. Let us not wonder at this, for in those days the spirit world was often more real to people than the present order.

I am continually amazed by the unwillingness of church people to believe in the miracles of the New Testament. They say that they cannot accept evidence of phenomena that would suggest the suspension of natural law. They have a limited epistemology and have reduced their faith to an inflexible positivism. Orthodox people, as W. R. Matthews has said, often make a serious mistake, thinking "they have all the truth and nothing more can be known."

As a matter of fact, wasn't the birth of Christ surrounded by the most supernatural of circumstances, including angelic visitation, voices from heaven, and a guiding star? Isn't the Christian faith established on the supernatural phenomena of an open grave and the bodily resurrection and appearance of the risen Lord? Wasn't the Christian church launched in the supernatural outpouring of wind, fire, and spirit-filled utterance? Didn't the Christian church come to the western world because of the supernatural experience of Paul, who saw a vision of a Macedonian man appealing to him: "Come over to Macedonia and help us?" (Acts 16:9.) Without belief in the supernatural power of God and the reality of the spiritual world, Christianity becomes a meaningless form.

During the past few years a tremendous interest has developed in the field of psychic research. In 1956 the

103

Spiritual Frontiers Fellowship was organized by a group of Christians representing several denominations. Some of these people are prominent churchmen, such as Sherwood Eddy, Arthur Ford, Alvin Bro, Marguerite Harmon Bro, Harmon Bro, Marcus Bach, Hornell Hart, Henry Smith Leiper, Roy Burkhart, Austin Pardue, and Ambrose Worrall—to name a few.

The older counterpart of this movement is The Church's Fellowship for Psychical Study, with headquarters in London, England. Membership in this organization includes twenty-two bishops in the Church of England, an archbishop, and such people as G. A. Chase, Oswald Jones, Leslie Weatherhead, Donald Soper, Leslie Newman, and many others.

Devoting themselves to careful inquiry and prayerful seeking, the Fellowships undertake study in the experience and interpretation of psychic and mystical manifestations; the practice and values of prayer; the evidence and the methodology of spiritual healing.

My mother once heard an old preacher say, "Perhaps it is better that Jesus did not tell us much about Heaven, for if he had told us all we might not want to go on living here." I firmly believe that if we could see into the next dimension we would be so eager to move on that we would want to leave this world without even saying "good-bye." Some people have reached the level of spiritual development where they can use Paul's words and truly mean them. "For me to live is Christ and to die is gain." (Phil 1:21.)

The late Glenn Clark, formerly a professor at Macalester College, once told of mailing a questionnaire to several students who had taken courses from him and after graduating from Macalester had made a significant contribution in their chosen work. One of the questions he asked of each person was: "Has there been a death in your immediate family?" Dr. Clark discovered that 99 percent of the people interviewed responded in the affirmative. An empty chair in the immediate family circle meant something to Glenn Clark. He claimed that the loved one who had gone ahead into the next life was able, by the power of the Holy Spirit, to release spiritual energy on those left behind that would sustain them and see them through the ordeal of grief and separation, by quickening their creative energies and preparing them to live productively in the days ahead.

My first reaction to this story was that of disbelief, but experience has taught me some lessons. Several women in our church have lost their husbands in the last few years, many of them with families to raise, debts to pay, and without adequate education and training to qualify for the sort of employment that would meet their financial needs. In each case these women have walked through the valley of the shadow of death and come out into the light of life with an incredible sustaining power.

One woman, who lost her thirty-six-year-old husband, was faced with the awesome responsibility of raising three young children alone. She is now doing what she would not or could not have done while her husband was alive. She is studying in a teachers' college, making excellent grades, and is on her way to getting her teacher's certificate. Another woman with three children lost her husband, who was in the real estate business. She has now

105

taken tests to qualify for selling real estate. Still another woman, whose husband died not long ago, was faced with the responsibility of raising a family alone, and is now self-employed in a successful baby-sitting enterprise. The stories go on and on.

In each case I have asked a searching question of these people left behind. How did you manage after your loved one died? The answers have been amazingly uniform. As one woman put it, "It seemed that my husband was right here telling me what to do; doors began to open and people have crossed my path who made the right suggestions and helped me at the opportune moment. I have the feeling that God has been absolutely taking over." God does not leave his people comfortless; he comes to them.

At Christmastime following the death of her husband, Mrs. John Williams, wife of the famous missionary to China, received a letter from fifteen young Chinese in Nanking who loved Dr. Williams and who had become Christians because of his witness for Christ. The letter contained a poem inspired by the Holy Spirit which must have set her heart on fire.

> Ye that have faith to look with fearless eyes
>> Beyond the tragedy of a world of strife,
> And trust that out of night and death shall rise
>> The dawn of ampler life;
> Rejoice, whatever anguish rend your heart,
>> That God has given you, for a priceless dower,
> To live in these great times and have your part
>> In freedom's crowning hour;

106

That ye may tell your sons who see the light
  High in the Heaven—their heritage to take—
"I saw the powers of darkness put to flight!
  I saw the morning break!" [1]

I must confess that I have not always felt a sense of assurance when reading the ritual for burial of the dead in the case of a person who has ignored the presence of God through most of his life. "Blessed are the dead who die in the Lord from henceforth: yea, saith the Spirit, that they may rest from the labors; and their works do follow them." Or, "Almighty God, with whom do live the spirits of those who depart hence in the Lord and with whom the souls of the faithful after death are in strength and gladness, we give thee hearty thanks for the good examples of all those thy servants."

There are times when I feel very much like the clergyman in the following story. When old Sam, the town drunkard, died, a few generous citizens of the community decided to give the old fellow a decent funeral. They purchased a cemetery lot, bought a casket, and secured the services of a local minister for the funeral. On the day of the ceremony the minister stood before the small gathering and said: "There isn't much I can say about Sam that you don't know already. He was drunk most of his life and never amounted to much, but as you pass by the open casket I want you to notice how good he looks since he stopped drinking."

[1] Owen Seaman, "Between Midnight and Morning," from *Masterpieces of Religious Verse* (New York: Harper & Row, 1948), p. 541. Copyright © *Punch* Magazine, London, used by permission.

Certainly I am not always convinced that the deceased is, as it says in the ritual, "in strength and gladness." When reading the ritual for a non-Christian I feel only a terrible wistfulness for anyone who enters the next life so far removed from the knowledge and experience of God, because they have not chosen him. However, I cannot impose my mental and spiritual limitations on Almighty God. His heart is infinitely larger than any of us can imagine. His judgment is sound and purposeful. Perhaps even in the midst of that dark place which is the final environment of self-love and self-worship there may be some way of salvation yet open to those who would repent. I cannot agree with a Jonathan Edwards' concept of judgment and hell as he was reported to have described it: "The God who holds you over the pit of hell, much as we hold a spider or some loathsome insect over the fire, abhors you and is dreadfully provoked. . . . You are ten thousand times so abominable in His eyes, as the most hateful and venomous serpent is in ours."

There are so many questions that remain unanswered about life and death, yet we possess an instinctive insight about the heart of God, and it must have been this deep knowing that caused Paul to include "life and death" among those things that are ours because of Christ.

In Marjorie Kinnan Rawlings' classic book *The Yearling,* there is recorded the unforgettable meditation of Penny, who was asked to say a few words at the burial of little Fodder-wing, the half-wit, cripple boy now lying in a fresh pine box. In simple, untutored language he speaks with eloquent perception.

108

Penny advanced to the grave and closed his eyes and lifted his face to the sunlight. The Forresters bowed their heads.

"Oh Lord. Almighty God. Hit ain't for us ignorant mortals to say what's right and what's wrong. Was ary one of us to be a-doin' of it, we'd not of brung this pore boy into the world a cripple, and his mind teched. We'd of brung him in straight and tall like his brothers, fitten to live and work and do. But in a way o' speakin', Lord, you done made it up to him. You give him a way with the wild creeturs. You give him a sort o' wisdom, made him knowin' and gentle. The birds come to him, and the varmints moved free about him, and like as not he could o' takened a she wild-cat right in his pore twisted hands.

"Now you've done seed fit to take him where bein' crookedy in mind or limb don't matter. But Lord, hit pleasures us to think now you've done straightened out them legs and that pore bent back and them hands. Hit pleasures us to think on him, movin' around as easy as ary one. And Lord, give him a few red-birds and mebbe a squirrel and a 'coon and a 'possum to keep him comp'ny, like he had here. All of us is somehow lonesome, and we know he'll not be lonesome, do he have them leetel wild things around him, if it ain't askin' too much to put a few varmints in Heaven. Thy will be done. Amen." [2]

Life and death, death and life, all moving in the same direction toward that inevitable rendezvous that cannot be postponed even for a moment.

---

[2] (New York: Charles Scribner's Sons, 1940), p. 197.

5

Present or the Future

The struggle of life itself is upward and ever upward.
—George Mallory

It was characteristic of Paul to affirm, "All things are yours . . . the present or the future." The live issue focuses attention on today and tomorrow. Yesterday is a dated résumé, kept in a filing case marked "reference." Indeed, the historical record can teach us valuable lessons, but we cannot live in the experiences of the past.

We face the future by facing each new day. We get to tomorrow by going through today and receiving from each passing moment all that God has there for us. We need to be expectant people whose lives are turned toward the rising sun, the daystar, the dawn, and the new day. It is today and tomorrow that matter; the direction of God's leading is always forward; it is never backward. People sometimes long for the good old days, when nearly everyone spent the entire Sabbath in church and practiced the old-time religion. We have heard folks say, "I wish I were still living back when folks were friendlier, grass was greener, and the sky bluer; when apples were juicier and kids were better mannered; when men told the truth and the gospel was preached with more power and persuasion." The hazy scene in the distant past will always look better to the man who can't stand his failures in the present. Strange how we glorify the yesterday because our today is miserable, and we don't have faith enough to receive the Holy Spirit and be led into a new day.

People with their faces turned toward yesterday take pleasure in dark, pessimistic sayings about today, and it has been so from ancient times. Long ago a man wrote, "Our earth is degenerated in these latter days. There are signs that the world is speedily coming to an end. Children no longer obey their parents. Every man wants to write a book. The end of the world is evidently approaching." These words were etched on an Assyrian tablet, dated from 2800 B.C. This sort of pessimism is a contemporary affliction visiting itself always on those who seek to hide themselves from the presence of the living God.

The chronological age of a person does not offer a valid criterion as to how pessimistic he may be concerning the present and the future. It was formerly held that only elderly people were the pessimists, but we are rapidly discovering that this enervating spirit crops up in other age groups as well. A certain man, after interviewing several college students on various campuses, was heard to remark, "College people today are pessimistic, conformed, dull, passive, unenthusiastic, unadventurous, and uncommitted." If this is true, it should be a matter of deep concern, because nothing can so stifle the creative spirit of a generation, paralyze its possibilities, and sap its strength as the mood of pessimism. And when this debilitating attitude gets into the churches, you find spirit-

111

ual death in the pulpit and pews. Perhaps the late French intellectual, Albert Camus, was speaking for more than he knew when he commented: "We are all of us alike in this. We are hostile to the past, indifferent to the present and hopeless as to the future."

But this is not the attitude of the mature Christian man or woman, no matter what his age or who he happens to be. Christianity, by the power of the Holy Spirit, has something to say and do about this sort of negative existence. There are those who are afraid to meet Jesus in the present moment. They lock him in a historical cell or push him off into a box marked, "Don't open until." But Jesus said, "I am," because the kingdom of God is.

The baptism of the Holy Spirit brings deep assurance to our souls. There is no more vacillation in our hearts, proceeding into our words. "I think I am a Christian." "I hope I am a Christian." "I guess I am a Christian." There are no more surmises and conditional guesses. There is only the full persuasion of the Holy Spirit's presence living within us. One of the evidences of the church's failure to emphasize the need for the baptism of the Holy Spirit is in the fact that thousands of church people do not speak for Jesus Christ, do not witness for him, do not lead in prayer, and do not speak to anyone else about the condition of their souls, because they are afraid of what other people might think of them. When the Holy Spirit fills a person, he becomes like Paul and Barnabas, who "spoke out boldly," or like Peter, who was a coward before "the maid who kept the door" in the temple courtyard, but who after Pentecost stood before

112

thousands of people in Jerusalem and fearlessly proclaimed Jesus Christ as Lord.

We need to remember Paul's words, "Do you not know that you are God's temple, and that God's Spirit dwells in you?" (I Cor. 3:16.) This is the word of God for our day, for the present and the future. Going before us into today and tomorrow, God sends his Holy Spirit to guide us, but we must stay close to him. Jesus told his followers, "When the Spirit of truth comes, he will guide you into all the truth; for he will not speak on his own authority, but whatever he hears he will speak, and he will declare to you the things that are to come" (John 16:13).

We should seek the guidance of the Holy Spirit as we begin each day. Communion is for the heart what guidance is for the feet. Communion is based upon our union with Christ. Where the Holy Spirit finds Christ in us, he finds the root of communion. If we begin each day with Christ, putting him at the center of our thoughts, allowing him the central place of our lives, then we shall be able to think his thoughts, share his interests, and join in his work. If, in the silence of our soul's chapel, we feel a holy prompting and are willing to be obedient to this guidance, then the leading of the Spirit will increase and grow into a very definite habit of our souls. We should claim the abiding presence of his Spirit and pray, "Lord, use me as you see fit, I give you my entire being and now await your orders. If I should be tempted to slip from thy guidance, please let me know before I fall too far. I am prepared to be led into the wilderness or into pleasant paths—I will follow the guidance you give me." Life in the Spirit is not an obscure, esoteric,

113

mystical condition; on the contrary, the Holy Spirit is exceedingly practical. He quickens our capabilities to grow, and above all to go from the defeats of today to the triumphs of tomorrow.

Paul was confident that, despite our human frailties, the Holy Spirit would see us through the present and the future. He said, "Likewise the Spirit helps us in our weakness; for we do not know how to pray as we ought, but the Spirit himself intercedes for us with sighs too deep for words" (Rom. 8:26).

We must stay close to our guide, the Holy Spirit. I have an agonizing remembrance of being separated from an Arab guide in the old city in Jerusalem. I wandered aimlessly through the crooked little streets of the holy city trying to find my only sure landmark, the Damascus gate. Without a guide, I was passing by famous historical and spiritual shrines with no idea as to what they were and where they were. I was moving through an enchanted world, filled with sacred meaning, walking where Jesus and the great biblical characters had walked, but with unseeing eyes because I had lost my guide. I will always remember that day because it vividly reminds me that no matter where you are, even while walking on holy ground, you still need guidance. The next day, while following a guide through Jerusalem, I had the wonderful experience of seeing the holy city that had been hidden to me the day before.

God confirms his guidance, but we must wait and listen for it. We need to pray, "Lord, do you want me to do this or not? Somehow let me know thy will." Guidance will come, and it will come strongly and positively if we are

114

tuned to listening. The Spirit leads us if we are willing to be led, but we must learn to distinguish between the voices of men and the voice of God. Unquestionably I have received godly guidance from other people, but there is real danger in trusting too much in the words of other men. We need to pray for spiritual hearing so sensitive that we will hear what Elijah heard—"a still small voice." There will come the great and mighty winds, rending the mountains, and shattering the rocks, but God will not be in the wind. There will come earthquakes, devastating in their upheaval and destruction, but the Lord will not be in the earthquakes; there will come fire, with smoke ascending to the sky, but the Lord will not be in the fire. Then at last the Lord spoke to Elijah, but he came, as Goodspeed translates, "in the sound of the gentle whisper" (I Kings 19:13).

We need to take a close look at Paul's expression, "all things are yours," as it applies to the present and the future. Certainly we cannot push back the future by putting off what must be done in the present. We cannot take possession of tomorrow until we have settled the account of today. God makes his appeal in the present, perhaps the uncomfortable present. He lays his sovereign claim on our lives, not "in a convenient season," but in the existential moment. Now is the acceptable time to receive him. Like Felix, the Roman governor of Caesarea, we have our moment of decision, when we cast our vote for tomorrow by what we do today. Standing in the council chamber of Governor Felix, Paul preached on faith in Jesus Christ to both Felix and his wife Drusilla, daughter of Herod Agrippa, who was actually the wife of another man, Felix having enticed her to live with him. Paul spelled out the implication of the gospel message in the present tense to the governor and his wife. He spoke of uprightness, self-control, and the coming judgment. Felix, twisting uneasily in his chair, was at length alarmed, and he said, "You may go for the present. When I find a convenient moment I will send for you again" (Acts 24:25, Phillips). The opportunity had come and gone. The answer Governor Felix gave Paul was not unlike the one many people, including churchmen, give the Holy Spirit.

The present does determine the future. What we do today sets the stage for tomorrow. One day I was studying my counseling program, and discovered that all the troubled, confused people coming to me for regular appointments over the past few weeks were those who gave little or nothing of themselves to the work of the Lord, privately or publicly. Their present holding back was blocking the channel of creative life and leaving their lives disturbed and empty.

The question for each Christian to ask himself is: "How much of myself am I giving away? Am I presently meeting the minimal standard of an invested life in Christ —through the tithe?" Anyone who seriously studies the Scriptures knows that God expects this from him. While Jesus did not say specifically that we must give a tenth of our income, he did say that he had come to fulfill the law. However, our response to Christ does not rest on the premise of law, but rather a relationship in love. The question of how much of our lives we shall invest in

Christ must be determined solely on the basis of our love for him.

Are we presently tithing our time? Today have we given time to practicing the presence of God, Bible study, and the study of Christian books? A missionary from Suriname, South America, told how the natives built their huts near the edge of the forest, and because the houses consist of only a single room, no one is able to withdraw to his own place of prayer. Therefore, the natives need to search for places in the forest near their homes that will serve as private places for daily prayer. One day the missionary overheard a Christian native shouting to his neighbor, "On your prayer path—I saw grass growing." Far too many Christians have lost their way because of the poorly kept prayer paths.

Are we presently tithing our strength in sacrificial service to others? Do we call on the sick, the lonely, the downcast? Have we taken time to make a telephone call today to someone in need or written a letter to cheer another person? At the very heart of the Christian faith is the cross. At Calvary someone flung a taunt at Jesus, "If you are the King of the Jews, save yourself!" But he could not. It is impossible for one who is saving others to save himself, and conversely, those who concentrate on saving themselves cannot save anyone else. If we are to live for Christ, we must die to self. The selfish, self-centered person, by attempting to save himself, robs himself of the greatest experience in life. He will never know the joy of spiritual growth nor the thrill of seeing life beyond the sensual dimensions.

Again we must come to grips with the divine formula,

"Give and it shall be given you." God is faithful; he will keep his laws. "The measure you give will be the measure you get." (Matt. 6:38.) You can't go your way selfishly saying, "Lord, I'll do this for you if you'll do this for me." If this is our attitude then we have broken the spirit of God's law and robbed ourselves of his glorious presence.

The essence of Christ's nature is self-giving love. On the human level this is nearly impossible; but it *is* possible if Christ's nature is living in us. In other words, we give of Christ what we have received of him, but you cannot give tomorrow what you have not received today. An old man said it well, "You can't give what you ain't got no more than you can come back from where you ain't been."

So the ability to meet the first criterion of the spiritual law of giving is to receive Jesus Christ into the center of our lives and be filled with his Spirit. We love because we have first been loved, and we give because we have first been given to. How many sins have you let Christ take away? How many problems have you let him solve? How many doors of your life have you opened to him in your social life, business life, family life, sex life, school life? How many sicknesses have you let him heal?

The present impinges on the future. Billy Graham speaks of an hour of decision. This may be your hour of decision, your moment of truth, your time to step forth into the laboratory of Christian faith and test its claims.

No one can satisfactorily tell another person how enormously fulfilling is the experience of receiving the Holy Spirit. Nor can you put into words the power that comes when you are witnessing to another about Christ, nor can you relate the tremendous rush of energy that

118

comes into a person when praying or reading the Holy Scriptures. The essential value of these spiritual disciples cannot be promoted from person to person as you would advertise a commodity and sell it through good public relations. We cannot talk people into growing spiritually, but we can invite and influence them toward the holy life by what they see of Christ in us.

A German pastor told of standing outside a famous cathedral that is reputed to be one of the most beautiful churches in the world. Gazing at the exterior of the building, he saw only the drab, dirty walls, the leaden gray windows, and the eroding signs of deterioration.

Then he stepped inside the cathedral, and immediately he saw the glorious color of the stained-glass windows and the internal loveliness of the old church. Later the pastor commented, "Seeing the beauty of this place depended entirely on whether I was inside the building or outside it." So it is with the spiritual life. You cannot know the glory of it until you are participating in the experience.

There is a heavy responsibility attached to the present moment of decision for Christ, and it is to receive to the fullest measure of our potential. A friend of mine is fond of saying, "Let's do it right now!" "Let's pray for this person right now." "Let's go see this person right now." "Let's read the Bible right now." Now is the acceptable time. Let us not go to more books, more conferences on prayer, more ministerial guidance, and more Christian friends. Let us go to God.

Paul's credo is stated in the following passage: "Brethren, I do not consider that I have made it my own; but one thing I do, forgetting what lies behind and strain-

119

ing forward to what lies ahead, I press on toward the goal for the prize of the upward call of God in Christ Jesus" (Phil. 3:13-14). Life begins to get into sharp focus when the eternal Christ lives within us. In this world of change and decay, frustration and doubt, the great apostle found the meaning of life toward which he could give the undivided loyalty of his heart. "One thing I do . . . I press on toward the goal." The present reality of Jesus Christ in his life gave him a sense of creative purpose, triumphant new life, joyous serenity, and dauntless faith. God is great enough to rule his mighty universe, but small enough to live within a man's heart.

Halford Luccock told of a village in the hills of Maine that was soon to be destroyed. It seems that the state had purchased all the land in that general area for the purpose of building a power dam, and the village rested on the site of a proposed lake. Once the people of the village learned of the dam project they were completely demoralized. Everything came to a stop. The village folk lost pride in the appearance of their community, and they even lost interest in one another. One man commenting said, "Where there is no faith in the future, there is no power in the present!"

As we have noted before, because of the uncertainty of world conditions, there is a tendency among many people to be unenthusiastic about the future. Skepticism, cynicism, indifference, and apathy have settled down on large numbers of people across the world. And yet there is a deep wistfulness in these people. Though they have no hope in the future, they still wish that they could hope. They are modern prodigals, homesick and lonely in a fantastically changing world. There is the prodigal businessman, goaded and pressured toward making a name for himself. There is the prodigal housewife and mother, escaping into feverish activity at home, school, club, and church. Young people reveal their own prodigalism through their assorted fears, frustrations, and rebellions. Prodigalism is always born in the despair of a powerless present while contemplating a hopeless future.

But the question still unanswered in the minds of prodigal people has to do with what their need really is. They are prodigal from God and do not know it. They have gone off into far countries searching to find the fulfillment that can only be found in the Father's house. They are like the famous geologist who kept ordering his assistants to lower him deeper and deeper into a crevice for better rock specimens. At evening time the muscles of the rope holders were so completely exhausted that when they tried to pull him up they could not lift him. It is hard to come back to God when you have said "no" to him so long. There is a dead weight in past refusal. I have found that the prodigalism in most people is a well-practiced habit of refusing to put oneself into the places where the power of God works most effectively. In their more honest moments prodigals will admit this, and at the moment any person in a far-off country "comes to himself"—through personal insight or with the help of another person—he will inevitably return to the Father's house, to be met, embraced, and welcomed back into the life of the household.

This is what causes witnessing for Christ to be of such vital importance. It becomes incumbent upon those who have found the way back to the Father's house to tell others the way. The hope we have for the world grows out of what we have found in the living presence of the Holy Spirit of God. Witnessing for Christ is not just a matter of doing good deeds. Rather, it is the proclamation of Jesus Christ in word and deed. Christian witnessing is not pleading a case or offering a devastating argument. Rather, it is stating your personal experience with Jesus Christ and seizing the initiative of each present moment to speak for your Lord. The ultimate question for all Christians is not how much understanding we have about Christ, but whether or not we know him. Therefore, when we witness we speak of what we know in Christ. As James Brown has said, "The Christian gospel is always within one generation of extinction." Our witness will keep the present alive in the future.

One day a man purchased a pair of shoes and, after returning home, discovered that he had not been charged the full amount of his purchase. A telephone call put him in contact with an elderly gentleman who had erred in his cash register accounting. He told the man that this sort of blunder could cost him his job, inasmuch as he was nearing the end of his years of service to the shoe company. The salesman thanked the man profusely when he volunteered to write a check for the unpaid balance. His words of appreciation were warm and sincere, though excessive in praise of the kind deed. At last the man said matter-of-factly, "The only reason I am sending you this money is because I am a Christian. Ten years ago I would have kept the money, considering myself fortunate to have profited by your mistake. However, because I have accepted Jesus Christ as my personal Savior I can do no other but write this check." Witnessing is a means of praising God and giving him all the glory.

A man I know with rare mechanical ability often stops to help people having automobile trouble along the side of the road. After he has worked on the car and has it running again people begin to express their appreciation by attempting to give him money as a token of gratitude. My friend always tells those whom he has helped, "Thank no one but God, I am just his servant." This sort of witness has a devastating effect on people. They do not seem to forget it.

There should be a definite strategy about our witnessing. We should intend to witness for Christ at any time and in any place. The thought uppermost in our minds when we are with people should be to speak a word for Christ.

Harry Denman, general secretary of evangelism for The Methodist Church, never carries a watch. Through a deliberate plan of action he goes about asking people, "What time is it?" so that he can engage them in conversation and eventually witness for Christ.

A salesman in our church carries a Bible on his appointed rounds, to read while waiting in a prospective client's outer office in full view of others who are likewise waiting. Many men and women are wearing "Yoke-fellow pins," replicas of small oxen yoke, which are the insignia of one particular spiritual life movement, or other pins of similar organizations. Invariably someone raises the question as to the meaning of the pin, and another opportunity for witness presents itself. The sight of business leaders reading their Bibles on a coffee break has a great effect on subordinate employees. The Christian housewife who lends a book on the Christian life to her neighbor will be offering a powerful witness.

A good friend of mine is pastor of the First Methodist Church in Green Bay, Wisconsin. Several of the Green Bay Packers' professional football team are members of his church. These men are faithful in church attendance, even on the day of a ball game. Though they may be involved in a crucial game, they are in church on Sunday morning, sitting calmly in their places, worshiping God. It would be difficult to erase from the memory of Green Bay church people the moving witness for God of a professional football player bowed in prayer before a big game. Witnessing occurs when we bow our heads in prayer in a public eating house, or when we tell a social friend about the importance of attending a prayer group, or when we invite our business associates to pray through a difficult problem.

Our hope for the future is rooted in the fact that men do respond to God in the present, no matter how far they have wandered from the Father's house. When we doubt that human nature can be redeemed, then we have no hope in the future and no power in the present.

Long ago I read how the shepherds of the holy land call their sheep that have wandered away and become lost in the mountains or valleys. The shepherds have learned that the earth will carry vibrations of sound over long distances, much farther than by air, if the vibrations are strong enough. So, when a sheep is lost, the shepherd climbs to the top of the highest hill and, after finding a deep crack in the rock, he blows his shepherd pipe down into the fissure. The earth picks up the sound and carries it through the hills and down into the valleys for miles in all directions. When the lost sheep feels the vibrations of the shepherd's call beneath his feet, he instinctively lifts his head to search the horizon of the highest hill—on top of which is his shepherd. From this experience no doubt the shepherd psalmist was inspired to write, "I will lift up my eyes to the hills, from whence does my help come?" (Ps. 121:1.) Christian people have their eyes on the great heights, though they may walk through the hopeless depths. They do not stumble because they have an ever-present guide—a shepherd who leads them on the way. It is this dauntless faith that we have in our Shepherd who "is the same yesterday and today and forever" (Heb. 13:8).

However, nothing in nature ever takes place in a haphazard way. Abiding law regulates all things. The Spirit of God comes upon people who are prepared to receive him. This fact may demolish the fond hope of many spiritually lazy people who have failed to make the effort to give themselves to a spiritual discipline. The conditions of spiritual law in Christ must be met in the present to insure a harvest in the future.

I received a letter from a young lady whose life longs for the abiding presence of the Holy Spirit. She writes a letter in two parts:

Part I

For the past three years I have been deeply searching for God, particularly this last year. I've tried everything

125

I know of, but without results. Desperate, though still trying, I was getting terribly discouraged but you and your church have given me hope—and maybe a wee bit more.

Concerning the things of the Spirit—I want to believe but my mind won't accept it completely. At present I think I believe it with my heart but not with my mind. I have been confused, and have felt despair and desolation. I have stood in the middle of a darkness blacker than the void of space, groping desperately for God, longing for Christ, and suffering an agony that the unquestioning cannot imagine. My God! Where can I turn? And the emptiness echoes my cry. Every once in awhile someone comes with a torch and says to me, "This is the way." I go toward them, but they are too fast for me and are soon gone; still I struggle toward where they disappeared. The blackness is unbearable. And then another light, another voice, but this time, another direction. How can I but go? Anything! Anything for the hope of finding God! But then it fades—and what now? Another comes and goes, and another. And I do not know whether I have gone in circles or if I am going somewhere, if I am nearer to my God, to reaching Him at last. This is not a dream, this is my life! And there are so many others with me, but all too many of them have grown to love the dark! Still there are many suffering as I suffer, and if I ever truly find God, (which I feel somehow certain now, that I will) I want with all my heart to help those others! Funny—I didn't start out to tell you this, but here it is—from the heart. I want to lead God's stumbling little children, but how can the blind lead the blind? I must first be made to see. I do not doubt that you know God, and I, though uncertain and afraid, want to know Him, too. I beg of you with every ounce of my being, help me! I am at the very, very end of my rope; I don't know what is left for me to do, but if you will help me, I will do whatever I must. Can you tell me what to do? Will you help me?

Part II

I am completely exhausted. I've been trying so hard; I am determined to live Christianity. I can't do it without God; in fact, I can't do anything I strive for without Him, and I realize that. I have recognized for some time that everything depends on whatever personal relationship I can establish with God. I've turned to the church, but its hypocrisy and insincerity revolt me. Then I turn—where? Where is there to turn? Nowhere! So I do nothing and become more desperately entangled in my own need.

But back to what I started out saying; Sunday afternoon after the worship service I felt that I was on the very brink of discovering God. I went to the healing service and knelt with the group at your church. I could not help joining them, though I felt terribly inadequate. It was an experience I'll never forget. God became real, and I prayed fervently that He would stay with me. I did not belong with that group, but surely some of their power and faith entered my being, unnoticed by me. For as we drove back home, I became aware of something burning within me, a great joy and sureness, and my burdens were lifted for a few marvelous hours. A taste of the Holy Spirit perhaps? I think it may have been. When we got home, I went directly to my youth group, and I was almost bursting with joy. If we had not had guests, I would have told the whole group. As it was, I told several people about what happened. After the movie we had, I had a sudden idea. I suggested to three girls that we start a prayer group! Since we accomplish practically nothing in our youth fellowship and I couldn't do anything about it (I tried several times) we have organized a group.

127

There are six and myself, and we're going to meet at my house Sunday at 3:30. We will pray, study, and investigate religion and prayer. I want to ask you and whoever you feel would help, to pray for us at that time. Would you? [1]

When we attempt to reach out and grab what we see of God's reckless good giving and try to tuck it away with the best of our souvenirs, we will soon learn that his gifts cannot be kept. They spoil when hoarded, they must be given away to be kept. He left his love behind in just that manner; we must choose his life in the present in order to live abundantly in the future. He was so sure— so incredibly sure—that somehow, some way we could not help following him off into the future, once we caught sight of him in the present.

After beholding the glory of the Lord, no wonder Paul could write, "All things are yours," and mean it.

[1] Used by permission.

128

G. DON GILMORE

G. Don Gilmore is minister of Groesbeck Methodist Church, Cincinnati, Ohio, where the church has grown tremendously under his vital leadership. A graduate of Wittenberg University (B.S.), and Garrett Theological Seminary (B.D.), he held student pastorates in Ohio and Illinois.

Mr. Gilmore is deeply interested in the Yokefellow movement and the Army of Compassion and Spiritual Frontiers Fellowship. Author of *In the Midst,* he is in great demand as an evangelistic speaker all over this country.